PRC Overseas Political Activities

Risk, Reaction and the Case of Australia

Andrew Chubb

www.rusi.org

Royal United Services Institute for Defence and Security Studies

PRC Overseas Political Activities: Risk, Reaction and the Case of Australia
First published 2021

Whitehall Papers series

Series Editor: Professor Malcolm Chalmers
Editor: Dr Emma De Angelis

RUSI is a Registered Charity (No. 210639)
Paperback ISBN [978-1-032-15207-3] eBook ISBN [978-1-003-24303-8]
Published on behalf of the Royal United Services Institute for Defence and Security Studies
by
Routledge Journals, an imprint of Taylor & Francis, 4 Park Square, Milton Park, Abingdon OX14 4RN

Image Credit: President Xi Jinping with Australia's Prime Minister Tony Abbott at Parliament House in Canberra, November 2014. *Courtesy of Reuters/Alamy Stock/ Lukas Coch*

SUBSCRIPTIONS
Please send subscription order to:

USA/Canada: Taylor & Francis Inc., Journals Department, 325 Chestnut Street, 8th Floor, Philadelphia, PA 19106 USA

UK/Rest of World: Routledge Journals, T&F Customer Services, T&F Informa UK Ltd, Sheepen Place, Colchester, Essex, C03 0LP UK

Contents

Acknowledgements   iv

About the Author   v

Introduction   1

    I.   **Conceptual Language: The Problem with 'Chinese Influence'**   14

    II.   **Disaggregating the Risks**   29

    III.   **Risks of Reaction: Australia's Experience with Aggregation**   54

    IV.   **Managing the Risks**   75

Conclusion: Two 'World Outlooks'   95

Acknowledgements

The author gratefully acknowledges support from the Columbia – Harvard China and the World Program and the Lowy Institute during this research project, and Emma De Angelis, Malcolm Chalmers, Veerle Nouwens, Zenab Hotelwala and the editorial team at RUSI. For helpful comments on earlier drafts, thanks in particular go to Geremie Barmé, David Brophy, David Campbell, Jie Chen, Tom Christensen, Mary Lynn de Silva, Gerry Groot, Ash Jones, Wendy Leutert, Darren Lim, Adam Ni, Alex Oliver, Charles Parton, Richard Rigby, Matthew Robertson, Wanning Sun, and all anonymous reviewers. Thanks are due also to those who kindly took the time to share their thoughts and ideas in formal interviews and informal conversations since the project's inception in 2017. The author takes sole responsibility for all shortcomings, errors and omissions.

About the Author

Andrew Chubb is a British Academy Postdoctoral Fellow based in the Department of Politics, Philosophy and Religion at Lancaster University, where he researches the linkages between China's domestic politics and international relations. A graduate of the University of Western Australia, his current project focuses on the role of domestic public opinion in international crisis diplomacy in the Asia-Pacific. More broadly, Andrew's interests include maritime and territorial disputes, strategic communication, political propaganda and Chinese Communist Party history. His recent research articles can be found in *International Security, International Relations of the Asia-Pacific* and *Asian Security.*

INTRODUCTION

The emergence of the People's Republic of China (PRC) as a global power has reanimated a central challenge for liberal democracies: how to protect both national security and political liberties when adversaries are willing and able to use one against the other. In President Xi Jinping's 'New Era' of PRC power, politicians, pundits and the media in the UK, the US and Australia are paying increasing attention to the overseas political activities of Beijing and its supporters. Many such concerns are well founded. Covert and overt political activities are in the Leninist DNA of China's ruling party, and communications technology has created new opportunities for authoritarian regimes to suppress dissent beyond their borders. On top of this, pro-Beijing patriots and wealthy lobbyists are advancing their views with increased confidence, and many influential economic actors involved in trade relations with China share significant overlapping interests with its party-state. Yet the need for policy responses to these developments also raises a further set of risks from within liberal democracies. These range from the polarisation of public discourse and the rise of alarmist rhetoric that fans xenophobia and harms social cohesion through to legislative encroachments on civil liberties and growing powers of national security agencies that operate with limited public oversight.

Such dilemmas are not new. The onset of the Cold War in the mid-20th century prompted painful choices and numerous missteps in liberal democracies. In the US, claims of widespread communist infiltration and subversion led to 'McCarthyist' political inquisitions and purges, along with legislation later deemed unconstitutional.[1] The UK and Australia both saw a major expansion in the largely unaccountable powers of security agencies that historians have argued generated little useful

---

[1] Landon R Y Storrs, 'McCarthyism and the Second Red Scare', *Oxford Research Encyclopedia of American History*, 2 July 2015, <https://oxfordre.com/americanhistory/view/10.1093/acrefore/9780199329175.001.0001/acrefore-97801 99329175-e-6>, accessed 8 June 2021; David Caute, *The Great Fear: The Anti-Communist Purge Under Truman and Eisenhower* (New York, NY: Touchstone, 1978).

intelligence.[2] Since the 1990s, and particularly after 2001, the ability of transnational terrorist groups to inflict mass fatalities – and potentially acquire weapons of mass destruction – prompted radical new security measures that encroached significantly on civil liberties and had debatable effectiveness in reducing the threat.[3] Most recently, in the age of social media, democracies have struggled to counter Russia's attempts to influence electoral processes, co-opt elites and suppress dissent by émigrés.[4] The overseas political activities of the PRC and its supporters present another expression of the ongoing challenge of protecting national security and democratic freedoms while preventing their abuse.

Debates on these policy dilemmas often frame liberty and security as being in tension, with an increase in one held to warrant a decrease in the other.[5] Yet recent experience has shown this assumption of inherent trade-offs does not always hold. During the Cold War, Australian security agencies mistakenly perceived causal linkages between foreign communism and activism on a wide array of issues – from Aboriginal rights and immigration policy to South African apartheid and the Vietnam War – leading to both encroachments on political freedoms and wastage of national security resources.[6] Post-9/11 attempts to strengthen national security have produced avoidable side effects affecting both liberty and security. Inflammatory political rhetoric on terrorism, for example, has undermined the government–community relations upon which effective security intelligence depends.[7] Sensationalist media and public commentary have stoked social division and Islamophobia by presenting Muslim communities as problem populations, while also amplifying the

---

[2] Keith Ewing, Joan Mahoney and Andrew Moretta, *MI5, the Cold War, and the Rule of Law* (Oxford: Oxford University Press, 2020); Keith Ewing, Joan Mahoney and Andrew Moretta, 'Cold War Redux: MI5, Russian Subversion and the Tory Government', *UK Constitutional Law Blog*, 8 September 2020; Meredith Burgmann (ed.), *Dirty Secrets: Our ASIO Files* (Sydney: NewSouth Publishing, 2014); John Blaxland, *The Protest Years: The Official History of ASIO 1963–1975* (Sydney: Allen & Unwin, 2016), especially Chapter 6.
[3] Jeremy Waldron, 'Security and Liberty: The Image of Balance', *Journal of Political Philosophy* (Vol. 11, No. 2, 2003), pp. 191–210.
[4] Intelligence and Security Committee of Parliament, *Russia*, HC 632 (London: Intelligence and Security Committee of Parliament, 2020).
[5] Waldron, 'Security and Liberty'; Mark Neocleous, 'Security, Liberty and the Myth of Balance: Towards a Critique of Security Politics', *Contemporary Political Theory* (Vol. 6, 2007), pp. 131–49.
[6] Blaxland, *The Protest Years*, p. 360.
[7] Malcolm Turnbull, *A Bigger Picture* (Melbourne: Hardie Grant, 2020), eBook version, Chapter 27; Duncan Lewis, 'Address to the Lowy Institute', 4 September 2019, <https://www.asio.gov.au/publications/speeches-and-statements/asio-director-general-address-lowy-institute.html>, accessed 22 March 2021.

sense of insecurity and mistrust among citizens more broadly. These experiences have highlighted the critical importance of the language and framing terminology used in policy debates, the need to draw sound analytic distinctions between issues, and the potentially harmful influence of elite political rhetoric and media coverage on the prospects for methodical, evidence-based public policymaking.

This paper examines the array of challenges the PRC's overseas political activities have presented to liberal democracies, as well as the significant risks involved in responding, drawing primarily on Australia's experience with both. This makes sense for two main reasons. First, Australia's regional proximity and relatively high level of economic and people-to-people engagement with the PRC have ensured a wide array of detailed examples are available, rendering many complex issues amenable to focused analysis. Second, since 2017 Australia has carried out an intense public policy debate on these issues, and Canberra has launched a series of policy initiatives accompanied by heavy publicity. These responses have been hailed internationally as a trailblazing model for countering foreign interference. Domestically controversial, Australia's policy responses have so far received little critical evaluation outside the country. This paper argues that Australia's experience offers cautionary lessons for other China-engaged liberal democracies.

The notion of engagement with China has come under heavy criticism as the PRC's domestic politics have become increasingly repressive.[8] From the 1990s onwards, successive governments in the US and the UK advanced the argument that expanding trade ties could help to liberalise the PRC. The Clinton administration drew rhetorically on this argument as it negotiated the PRC's entry into the World Trade Organization.[9] New Labour under then Prime Minister Tony Blair likewise claimed that trading with China would help promote internal liberalisation.[10] A 2009 Foreign Office report laid out 15 ways that the UK was seeking to promote 'sustainable development, modernisation and internal reform in China'.[11] Whether or not such goals were plausible (or

---

[8] Kurt M Campbell and Ely Ratner, 'The China Reckoning: How Beijing Defied American Expectations', *Foreign Affairs* (Vol. 97, No. 2, March/April 2018); Alastair Iain Johnston, 'The Failures of the "Failure of Engagement" with China', *Washington Quarterly* (Vol. 42, No. 2, 2019), pp. 99–114.

[9] Neil Thomas, 'Matters of Record: Relitigating Engagement with China', MacroPolo, 3 September 2019, <https://macropolo.org/analysis/china-us-engagement-policy>, accessed 22 March 2021.

[10] Shaun Breslin, 'Beyond Diplomacy? UK Relations with China Since 1997', *British Journal of Politics and International Relations* (Vol. 6, No. 3, 2004), pp. 409–25.

[11] Charles Parton, 'Towards a UK Strategy and Policies for Relations with China', King's College London Policy Institute, June 2020, p. 11.

sincerely pursued) at the time, it has become clear that the PRC has moved in the opposite direction domestically, while its capabilities and interests outside its own borders have expanded markedly. These developments are increasing the political salience of PRC overseas political activities in the national security discourses of many liberal democracies. Given growing Sino-American security tensions, this is likely to intensify further, particularly for US-aligned states such as the UK.

The UK's relations with the PRC have deteriorated significantly since David Cameron and George Osborne, respectively UK prime minister and chancellor of the exchequer, flagged a 'golden era' of bilateral ties in 2015. Controversy over PRC telecoms giant Huawei's potential involvement in the UK's 5G network, Beijing's abrogation of treaty commitments to maintain Hong Kong's autonomy and freedoms, and extreme repression of ethnic and religious groups have placed ties under increasing strain. There is broad political momentum behind tougher stances constraining scientific and technological cooperation in areas with potential military relevance, and on human rights abuses such as the mass internment of Uyghur Muslims in re-education camps. A significant number of Conservative MPs now advocate a generalised rollback of economic cooperation with the PRC and an overarching policy aimed at countering the PRC's influence around the world.[12] In response, Prime Minister Boris Johnson has vowed to 'be tough on some things, but also … to continue to engage'.[13] Finding this balance is likely to be increasingly challenging in the coming years.

As the PRC becomes an increasingly global power, engagement is neither an inherent good nor a general threat to be avoided or eliminated. It is, instead, a reality of today's world. The UK's 2021 *Integrated Review of Security, Defence, Development and Foreign Policy* assessed China's rise as 'by far the most significant geopolitical factor in the world today'.[14] Given the PRC's economic and political footprints, its growing military power in the world's most economically vibrant region, and its importance in global crises such as climate change and the coronavirus pandemic, ongoing engagement with the PRC across a range of sectors is both necessary and inevitable, irrespective of any view of the

---

[12] Ben Judah, 'Transcript: U.K.-China Clash: A Conversation with Sir Iain Duncan Smith MP', Hudson Institute, 9 July 2020, <www.hudson.org/research/16209-transcript-u-k-china-clash-a-conversation-with-sir-iain-duncan-smith-mp>, accessed 22 March 2021.

[13] Rob Merrick, 'Boris Johnson Says UK Must "Continue to Engage with China" and Hints Sanctions Unlikely', *The Independent*, 20 July 2020.

[14] HM Government, *Global Britain in a Competitive Age: The Integrated Review of Defence, Development and Foreign Policy*, CP 403 (London: The Stationery Office, 2021), p. 62.

appropriate volume and nature of economic cooperation. As Charles Parton notes, a blanket policy of disengagement would serve no discernible purpose.[15] Rather than engagement itself, it is the specific forms of engagement with the PRC across different sectors that merit debate. Even if a general 'decoupling' was possible, the PRC – and the overseas political activities examined in this paper – would remain a reality with which democracies must grapple. As Australian writer and translator Linda Jaivin surmises: 'Ready or not, China is here'.[16]

An Australian Microcosm

In December 2017, voters in Australia's federal parliamentary seat of Bennelong went to the polls in a crucial by-election. A loss for the Liberal party would have eliminated its one-seat majority in parliament, potentially bringing an end to Prime Minister Malcolm Turnbull's Liberal-National coalition government. The vote had been triggered by the revelation that the incumbent MP was a foreign citizen, and debate duly raged throughout the campaign over foreign influence in the Australian parliament. But the foreign power at the centre of controversy was not the one to which the MP owed allegiance – the UK – but the country's largest trading partner, China.

During the two-week campaign, media reports and commentary suggested Beijing was mobilising political proxies and propaganda to influence the result.[17] For one prominent commentator, Bennelong represented nothing less than an attempt by Beijing to engineer a change of government in Canberra.[18] Amid this heated electoral rhetoric, the government tabled new legislation to counter foreign political interference, with Turnbull channelling Chairman Mao Zedong by declaring in mangled Mandarin: 'The Australian people have stood up'.[19]

---

[15] Parton, 'Towards a UK Strategy', p. 6; see also Sophia Gaston and Rana Mitter, 'After the Golden Age: Resetting UK-China Engagement', British Foreign Policy Group, July 2020.

[16] Linda Jaivin, 'The New Era: Ready or Not, China is Here', *The Monthly*, December 2017, <www.themonthly.com.au/issue/2017/december/1512046800/linda-jaivin/new-era>, accessed 22 March 2021.

[17] Nick O'Malley and Alex Joske, 'Mysterious Bennelong Letter Urges Chinese Australians to "Take Down" the Turnbull Government', *Sydney Morning Herald*, 13 December 2017; Alex Joske, 'Bennelong Byelection: The Influential Network Targeting the Turnbull Government in Bennelong', *Sydney Morning Herald*, 15 December 2017.

[18] Clive Hamilton, *Silent Invasion: China's Influence in Australia* (Melbourne: Hardie Grant, 2018), pp. 53–54.

[19] Christopher Knaus and Tom Phillips, 'Turnbull Says Australia Will "Stand Up" to China as Foreign Influence Row Heats Up', *The Guardian*, 9 December 2017.

More than 20% of voters in Bennelong are of Chinese origin, much higher than the national average of 5.6%.[20] This made Bennelong's Chinese communities an important target for Australia's two major parties – and potentially also for the Chinese Communist Party (CCP). The Labor opposition, already reeling from the resignation of a senator over a series of scandals involving PRC political donors, accused the government of 'China-phobic rhetoric'.[21] Meanwhile, in Beijing, propaganda organs denounced Australia's 'hysterical paranoia, full of racial undertones'.[22] For the first time in decades, China had become a political football in an Australian electoral contest, as well as a potential player.

As it turned out, the government comfortably retained the seat, and evidence of PRC interference was weak.[23] One influential pro-Beijing figure

---

[20] Australian Bureau of Statistics, '2016 Census QuickStats', 23 October 2017, <https://quickstats.censusdata.abs.gov.au/census_services/getproduct/census/2016/quickstat/CED103>, accessed 21 March 2021.

[21] O'Malley and Joske, 'Mysterious Bennelong Letter'.

[22] Nick O'Malley and Alex Joske, 'Claims of Chinese Influence, Betrayal and Racism on the Streets of Bennelong', *Sydney Morning Herald*, 11 December 2017; Bill Birtles, Steven Viney and Xiaoning Mo, 'China Slams Malcolm Turnbull's "Hysterical, Racist Paranoia"; *ABC News*, Anniversary Unlikely to Mend Relations', 12 December 2017; Zhong Sheng, '澳方对华认知须从事实出发' ['Australia's Understanding of China Should Start With Facts'], *Renmin Ribao* [*People's Daily*], 11 December 2017, <https://opinion.people.com.cn/n1/2017/1211/c1003-29696952.html>, accessed 21 March 2021.

[23] The key piece of evidence cited to suggest PRC interference was an anonymous letter that appeared on social media platform WeChat on December 13, urging Chinese-Australians to use their votes to bring an end to the Turnbull government. Australian-based Chinese-language media reporting indicates it was the initiative of Yan Zehua, a Chinese citizen and long-term resident of Australia, who is deputy director of the Australian Council for the Promotion of the Peaceful Reunification of China (ACPPRC), a CCP-affiliated umbrella organisation for the Beijing-friendly United Front community groups. However, the letter does not appear to have circulated widely on Chinese social media, as would be expected if it had state backing. Coverage by the Beijing-friendly online news outlet *Sydney Today*, for example, appears to have been prompted by English-language Australian media reporting rather than the original letter itself. The outlet's online report contained only the partial image of the letter posted by Fairfax Media, suggesting it had not been shared widely enough to come to the attention of the outlet's editors via Chinese social media. Yan claims he has generally supported the Australian Labor Party since the Bob Hawke government granted him permanent residency following the 1989 Beijing massacre. See Chen Hong, '華人社團領袖籲投工黨　斥譚保政府損華人利益' ['Chinese Community Leader Calls for Voting Labor, Accuses Turnbull Government of Harming Chinese People's Interests'], *Xingdao Ribao* [*Sing Tao Daily*], 14 December 2017. A study of 318 WeChat articles on Australia's 2019 election found the coverage to be biased towards the incumbent conservative party. See Fan Yang and Fran Martin, 'The 2019 Australian Federal Election on WeChat Official Accounts: Right-Wing

with strong ties to the CCP overseas propaganda system publicly backed the incumbent.[24] But six months later, the government invoked the spectre of foreign interference in the by-election to push through a far-reaching, complex and deeply controversial cluster of national security laws.[25]

Bennelong was a microcosm of the storms buffeting US-aligned, China-engaged liberal democracies over the political activities of the CCP and its supporters, against the backdrop of rising geopolitical tensions. Debates in Australia have raged between two poles of argument. At one end are suspicions regarding the political activities of PRC-aligned businesses, political donors, lobbyists, diaspora groups and overseas students. At the other, there are concerns about the consequences of inflammatory public rhetoric, hasty legislative responses and encroachments on civil liberties in multicultural democratic societies with histories of racism and anti-Chinese sentiment. Navigating this collision of concerns is the purpose of this paper.

The CCP Overseas in Xi Jinping's 'New Era'

As Australia geared up for the Bennelong by-election, the PRC was grappling with the implications of the 19th Congress of the Chinese Communist Party. In a 205-minute speech to the meeting, Xi had heralded an epochal shift for China and the world. Prostrate until 1949, and poor through much of the 20th century, the PRC was already becoming prosperous when he took charge in 2012. Now a new era of PRC power had arrived.[26]

Dominance and Disinformation', *Melbourne Asia Review* (No. 5, 2021), <https://melbourneasiareview.edu.au/the-2019-australian-federal-election-on-wechat-official-accounts-right-wing-dominance-and-disinformation>, accessed 22 March 2021.

[24] Nick McKenzie and Alex Joske, 'Chinese Media Mogul Tommy Jiang Wants John Alexander in Bennelong', *Sydney Morning Herald*, 15 December 2017.

[25] Attorney-General Christian Porter touted an 'unprecedented' threat of interference to argue the legislation had to be passed before a series of by-elections. See John Power, 'Australia's Spy Law Revamp Irks China', *Nikkei Asia*, 20 June 2018; Simon Benson, 'Foreign Interference "Threat" to By-Elections, Says Christian Porter', *The Australian*, 8 June 2018, <https://www.theaustralian.com.au/nation/foreign-interference-threat-to-byelections-says-christian-porter/news-story/a0aa4f6577af71bf5b4456dd7ea14f64>, accessed 21 March 2021; Gareth Hutchens, 'Coalition Pressures Labor to Urgently Pass Spy Laws to Avert "General Chaos" at Byelections', *The Guardian*, 10 June 2018.

[26] Xi Jinping, 'Secure a Decisive Victory in Building a Moderately Prosperous Society in All Respects and Strive for the Great Success of Socialism with Chinese Characteristics for a New Era', speech at the 19th National Congress of the Communist Party of China, Beijing, 18 October 2017, *Xinhua*, 18 October 2017; Darren Lim and Victor Ferguson, 'Power in Chinese Foreign Policy', in Jane

China has become the world's biggest trading and manufacturing economy, second in the world for GDP, incoming Foreign Direct Investment (FDI) and commodity consumption. It is also the largest holder of foreign exchange reserves, as well as possessing the world's most sophisticated surveillance state and an increasingly powerful military.[27] Considerable influence would naturally accompany such economic, technological and military heft. But Xi's declaration signalled that his party-state apparatus would wield its power with increased vigour in the future.

Covert and overt attempts at exerting political influence overseas are in the party's DNA – not because it is Chinese, but because it is an unreformed and increasingly dictatorial Leninist party-state.[28] The ongoing prominence of Lenin's ideas in the CCP's approach to politics is primarily manifest in the party's ongoing organisational penetration of key political and economic institutions, which has been stepped up significantly in recent years.[29] Leninism is also reflected in the party's United Front work (see Chapter I), which aims to control and direct actors outside the party to advance CCP goals.[30]

Golley et al. (eds), *China Story Yearbook 2018: Power* (Canberra: ANU Press, 2019), pp. 55–59.

[27] State Council Information Office of the People's Republic of China, 'White Paper: China and the World in the New Era', 27 September 2019.

[28] Steve Tsang, 'Consultative Leninism: China's New Political Framework', *Journal of Contemporary China* (Vol. 18, No. 62, 2009), pp. 866–68; James Jiann Hua To, *Qiaowu: Extra-Territorial Policies for the Overseas Chinese* (Leiden: Brill, 2014).

[29] Built up before and after 1949, torn down during the Cultural Revolution, and relatively restrained in many areas of economy and administration between 1978 and the early 2000s, the CCP's Leninist organisational apparatus has been reinvigorated in recent years. See Richard McGregor, *The Party: Inside the Secret World of China's Rulers* (New York, NY: HarperCollins, 2010).

[30] For a succinct and recent summary of the CCP United Front Work Department's scope and structure, see James Kynge, Lucy Hornby and Jamil Anderlini, 'Inside China's Secret "Magic Weapon" for Worldwide Influence', *Financial Times*, 26 October 2017; on the general nature of the United Front's work, see Kumar Ramakrishna, 'Original Sin'?: Revising the Revisionist Critique of the Operation Coldstore in Singapore* (Singapore: ISEAS, 2015), pp. 25–26; for a detailed historical treatment of the United Front's work, see Gerry Groot, *Managing Transitions: The Chinese Communist Party, United Front Work, Corporatism and Hegemony* (New York, NY: Routledge, 2004); on more recent developments in the United Front's work, see Gerry Groot, 'The Expansion of the United Front Under Xi Jinping', in Gloria Davies, Jeremy Goldkorn and Luigi Tomba (eds), *The China Story Yearbook 2015: Pollution* (Canberra: ANU Press, 2016), pp. 167–77; Gerry Groot, 'United Front Work After the 19th Party Congress', *China Brief* (Vol. 17, No. 17, 2017); Peter Mattis and Alex Joske, 'The Third Magic Weapon: Reforming China's United Front', *War on the Rocks*, 24 June 2019; Alex Joske,

In contrast with Lenin's Soviet Union, however, the PRC today does not seek to engineer a global revolution. The CCP's official self-ascribed role has explicitly shifted from a revolutionary party to a governing one.[31] Chinese companies have, in recent years, begun to export technologies that help authoritarian states monitor populations and suppress dissent.[32] But since the end of the Mao era, the PRC has shown little interest in spreading its political system to foreign countries.

Today, the PRC's overseas political activities aim to narrow and shape how China-related issues are discussed. Beijing – and some of its supporters overseas – specifically seeks to stifle criticism of, and opposition to, the PRC's leaders, the single-party system, its human rights record and China's positions on territorial issues and other contentious foreign policy matters.[33] The advancement of such goals, and the methods deployed in their pursuit, present a complex array of challenges for liberal democracies that have become more acute as the PRC's power and international presence have grown.

How do the PRC and its supporters advance their political interests outside China's borders? Are such activities effective? Are they substantively different from those of others working to advance political agendas? Do they threaten the sovereignty, civil liberties and academic institutions of liberal democracies – and if so, how – and what should be the response? This paper argues that answering these questions depends on carefully distinguishing between the issues in question.

'The Party Speaks for You: Foreign Interference and the Chinese Communist Party's United Front System', Australian Strategic Policy Institute, June 2020.

[31] Timothy Heath, *China's New Governing Party Paradigm: Political Renewal and the Pursuit of National Rejuvenation* (London: Ashgate, 2014).

[32] Tin Hinane El Kadi, 'The Promise and Peril of the Digital Silk Road', Chatham House, 6 June 2019, <www.chathamhouse.org/expert/comment/promise-and-peril-digital-silk-road>, accessed 9 July 2021; Paul Mozur, Jonah Kessel and Melissa Chan, 'Made in China, Exported to the World: The Surveillance State', *New York Times*, 24 April 2019; in his Work Report to the 19th Party Congress, Xi stated that the 'New Era' 'means that the continuous development of the road, theory, system and culture of Socialism with Chinese Characteristics has opened up a route for developing countries to move towards modernization, providing an entirely new choice to those of the world's countries and nations that hope to both accelerate development and maintain their own independence, contributing Chinese wisdom and Chinese plans towards the resolution of humankind's problems'. Xi, 'Secure a Decisive Victory'.

[33] Jessica Chen Weiss, 'A World Safe for Autocracy? China's Rise and the Future of Global Politics', *Foreign Affairs*, July/August 2019, pp. 92–102; John Fitzgerald, 'Mind Your Tongue: Language, Public Diplomacy and Community Cohesion in Contemporary Australia–China Relations', Australian Strategic Policy Institute, 2019.

Aggregation versus Disaggregation

Responding effectively to the challenges presented by the PRC's overseas political activities starts with disaggregating the distinct risks they pose. Only some threaten the security and the integrity of democratic political systems; many more impinge instead on the rights and freedoms of individual residents.[34] Others still undermine academic freedom – the particular set of freedoms central to the functioning of liberal educational institutions. Importantly, however, numerous controversial pro-PRC activities are in fact normal exercises of liberal-democratic rights.

The sources of risk vary considerably. While some have arisen with the PRC's increasingly authoritarian direction at home and growing coercive capabilities abroad, many are primarily a matter of deficiencies in democracies' own political and legal institutions. Others result from the growth of the Chinese economy and international trade, which has generated overlapping economic interests between the party-state, international businesses and foreign governments and constituencies. At the same time, close examination of Australia's policy responses highlights a further set of risks, including alarmist public discourse, legislative overreach and institutional mismatches, that can arise from within democracies themselves as a result of the need to respond. Taking account of these distinct sets of risks is a prerequisite for the development of methodical, comprehensive liberal-democratic policy responses.

The disaggregation-based approach suggested here contrasts with the aggregation of issues into an overarching national security threat – attributed to the CCP, but with a scope of participation extending far beyond the party – and commonly termed 'Chinese influence'.[35] Proponents of aggregation argue that viewing the full array of authoritarian threats to liberal democracy through a national security lens is important to overcome political inertia and mobilise coordinated action among democracies.[36] However, aggregation carries significant drawbacks.

---

[34] Samantha Hoffmann and Peter Mattis, 'China's Incursion on American Campuses Is Nothing to Take Lightly', *The Hill*, 3 May 2018.

[35] Larry Diamond and Orville Schell (eds), 'Chinese Influence and American Interests: Promoting Constructive Vigilance', Hoover Institution, 2018; Jonas Parello-Plesner, 'The Chinese Communist Party's Foreign Interference Operations: How the U.S. and Other Democracies Should Respond', Hudson Institute, 2018; Clive Hamilton, *Silent Invasion*. The most thorough critique of the latter book is David Brophy, 'Review of *Silent Invasion: China's Influence in Australia*', *Australian Book Review* (No. 400, April 2018).

[36] Laura Rosenberger and John Garnaut, 'The Interference Operations from Putin's Kremlin and Xi's Communist Party: Forging a Joint Response', *Asan Forum*, 8 May 2018; Christopher Walker and Jessica Ludwig, 'From "Soft Power" To "Sharp Power":

First, attributing a wide array of issues to CCP malign activity risks misdiagnosing their causes while simultaneously exaggerating the party's power. If a foreign state's actions or intentions are taken as the cause of problems that are in fact rooted in more general systemic shortcomings, such as the influence of money in politics, or obstacles to full political participation by particular social groups, such vulnerabilities are likely to remain unaddressed in policy responses. Inflating an authoritarian regime's existing overseas capability can be counterproductive, aiding its efforts to intimidate émigré communities and potentially creating bandwagon effects. As the Soviet dissident Alexander Zinoviev sardonically wrote, 'People are more ready to help an omnipotent enemy than a weak friend'.[37]

Second, expanding the umbrella of national security tends to preclude the transparency and careful deliberation among competing values necessary for an effective liberal-democratic response. The term 'national security' invokes the special gravity of the state's survival to justify suspension of the normal rules of political contestation in a democratic society.[38] Accordingly, security agencies are permitted to operate with lower standards of public accountability and scrutiny than other government institutions. This has been accepted where defence, espionage and the integrity of the political system are concerned. However, broadening the scope of national security and expanding the powers of domestic security agencies may be methods ill-suited to tasks such as protecting diaspora communities' democratic rights and conducting informed public policy debates (see Chapter III).

Third, rolling the PRC's overseas political activities together into an overarching security frame can harm the pursuit of broader national interests. Diminished economic exchanges are not the only opportunity cost of overly broad securitisation. Implicating large groups of people as potentially suspect has negative consequences for social cohesion, a critical source of strength for multicultural liberal democracies.[39] Experience with counterterrorism in recent decades has

---

Rising Authoritarian Influence in the Democratic World', in Juan Pablo Cardenal et al., *Sharp Power: Rising Authoritarian Influence* (Washington, DC: National Endowment for Democracy, 2017), pp. 8–25.

[37] Alexander Zinoviev, *Homo Sovieticus* (London: Victor Gollancz, 1985), p. 70.

[38] Barry Buzan et al., *Security: A New Framework for Analysis* (London: Lynne Reinner, 1998), p. 29; in an early essay on the subject, Arnold Wolfers noted that national security policies imply 'subordinat[ion of] other interests to those of the nation'. See Arnold Wolfers, '"National Security" as an Ambiguous Symbol', *Political Science Quarterly* (Vol. 67, No. 4, 1952), p. 481.

[39] Gordon de Brouwer, 'Risk Management When Security, Economics Collide', *East Asia Forum Quarterly* (Vol. 11, No. 4, 2019), pp. 3–4.

demonstrated the importance of government–community relations to security.[40] Australia's Counter Foreign Interference Strategy explicitly lists a 'multicultural, cohesive and open society' as a key strength in countering foreign interference.[41] Avoiding overblown public discourse that fans Sinophobia and generalised suspicions of large groups of people, then, is also a matter of national security.

The contrasting analytic approaches of aggregation and disaggregation point to divergent policy approaches. Aggregation of issues under a national security umbrella points to an urgent campaign to wrest democracies' politics, business, academia and diasporas free from the grip of extant CCP control. Advocates of aggregation have argued that defending democracy requires 'decisive action to counter [the CCP] across the board',[42] and the excision of pernicious 'Chinese influence' from the body politic.[43] From their perspective, policy should be assessed by its effectiveness in suppressing pro-CCP activities,[44] victories in 'political warfare'[45] and, for some, civilisational struggle.[46] The analysis in this paper points instead to a differentiated set of measures designed

---

[40] Allan Gyngell and Darren Lim, 'Ex-ASIO Head Duncan Lewis (Part 2): Foreign Interference and National Security Policymaking in Australia', *Australia in the World* Podcast, Episode 36, 19 December 2019, <australiaintheworld.podbean. com/e/ep-36-ex-asio-head-duncan-lewis-part-2-foreign-interference-and-national-security-policymaking-in-australia>, accessed 22 March 2021.

[41] Australian Government, Department of Home Affairs, 'Australia's Counter Foreign Interference Strategy', 22 January 2020.

[42] Robert O'Brien, 'The Chinese Communist Party's Ideology and Global Ambitions', speech given in Phoenix, Arizona, 24 June 2020, <https://china. usembassy-china.org.cn/the-chinese-communist-partys-ideology-and-global-ambitions/>, accessed 17 March 2021.

[43] Clive Hamilton, 'Labor Has a Cancer Growing in it that Must Be Cut Out', *Sydney Morning Herald*, 19 February 2018.

[44] Clive Hamilton and Alex Joske's 2018 parliamentary submission argued that relevant Australian legislation should be measured by 'how well it suppresses united front activities in Australia'. See Clive Hamilton and Alex Joske, 'Submission to the Parliamentary Joint Committee on Intelligence and Security', Inquiry into the National Security Legislation Amendment (Espionage and Foreign Interference) Bill 2017, 22 January 2018, p. 2.

[45] Andrew Hastie, 'What Is to Be Done?', in Andrew Foxall and John Hemmings (eds), 'The Art of Deceit: How China and Russia Use Sharp Power to Subvert the West', Henry Jackson Society, 2019; see also Clive Hamilton's recommendations at the conclusion of Hugh White, Clive Hamilton and Rebecca Strating, 'Does China Pose a Threat to Australia? What Should Our China Policy Be?', *Ideas & Society* podcast, La Trobe University Clever Conversations, 6 March 2019, <www. latrobe.edu.au/news/clever-conversations/ideas-and-society/livestream/does-china-pose-a-threat-to-australia>, accessed 22 March 2021.

[46] David Wroe, 'Defending Democracy a Generational Struggle, Australian MPs Warn', *Sydney Morning Herald*, 10 July 2018.

methodically to eliminate, minimise or mitigate each particular risk identified. It advocates a risk-management framework that takes the preservation and strengthening of three core liberal-democratic institutions – integrity of the political system, protection of civil rights of individuals and groups, and academic freedom in research and education – as the immediate and overriding goal of policy measures.

Scope and Structure

The scope of this paper is limited to PRC overseas political activities, defined here as 'activities that influence or attempt to influence political discussions or processes outside China's borders' and discussed in further detail in Chapter I. Despite the diversity of the issues discussed, they constitute only one aspect of any general China policy agenda, which would include issues such as geopolitics, multilateral diplomacy, cyber security, investment, trade, research collaboration, and technology and industry policies, among others. The complexity of engagement with the PRC, and with the Chinese world more broadly, means evaluation of these other important policy areas will lie beyond the scope of this paper. One point it does attempt to demonstrate decisively, however, is that there exists no contradiction between taking seriously the risks raised by the PRC's overseas political activities and taking seriously the risks involved in responding.

Chapter I clarifies the terms used in English-language debates concerning PRC overseas political activities, detailing why accurate terminology is key to both diagnosis of problems and policy outcomes. Chapter II unpacks the bundle of activities commonly labelled 'Chinese influence' into three distinct risk areas – national security; civil rights; and academic freedom – identifying significant variation in their causes, impact and relationship to liberal-democratic principles. Chapter III critically evaluates Australia's response to PRC political activities, illustrating the risks of national security aggregation as an analytic approach and a basis for public policy responses. Chapter IV suggests a set of policy measures designed to simultaneously strengthen national security, civil rights and academic freedom in liberal democracies in the context of the PRC's growing international political and economic clout. The Conclusion returns to the broad question of the relationship between security and liberty, highlighting the need for governments, analysts and commentators to avoid the trap of implicitly adopting the CCP's conspiratorial view of politics.

I. CONCEPTUAL LANGUAGE: THE PROBLEM WITH 'CHINESE INFLUENCE'

Accurate definition of problems is crucial to the development of effective policy responses. In his 1946 essay 'Politics and the English Language', George Orwell made an impassioned plea for precision in political discourse against a proliferation of vague and malleable set phrases.[1] In national security policy, amorphous concepts such as the 'communist threat' during the Cold War and 'terrorism' after 9/11 have hindered rational assessment of the nature and magnitude of threats.[2] Choice of language influences how the qualitative nature of a problem is understood, along with the causes that give rise to it, the broader associations that audiences will draw and the design of public policy solutions.[3] Unfortunately, the basic terms in which the CCP and its supporters' political activities have been discussed in English have been frequently vague and potentially misleading. As Chapter III will argue, such imprecision has contributed to unwarranted and often unintended associations between state conduct and ethnicity, misidentification of priorities for policy responses, and missed opportunities to strengthen liberal-democratic institutions.

---

[1] George Orwell, 'Politics and the English Language', *Horizon*, April 1946.
[2] Arnold Wolfers, a pioneer in the field of security studies, stressed the importance of clarity and precision regarding threats to national security: 'It would be an exaggeration to claim that the symbol of national security is nothing but a stimulus to semantic confusion', he wrote in 1952, 'though closer analysis will show that if used without specifications it leaves room for more confusion than sound political counsel or scientific usage can afford'. See Wolfers, '"National Security" as an Ambiguous Symbol', p. 483. See also David Baldwin, 'The Concept of Security', *Review of International Studies* (Vol. 23, No. 1, 1997), pp. 5–26, especially pp. 12–18.
[3] David A Rochefort and Roger W Cobb (eds), *The Politics of Problem Definition: Shaping the Policy Agenda* (Lawrence, KS: University of Kansas Press, 1994), pp. 1–31.

This chapter examines the concepts deployed in English-language discussions on the PRC's overseas political activities. The first section discusses the ambiguities of the English-language term 'Chinese influence', showing how, deployed to describe problematic or nefarious PRC political activities, it is likely to exaggerate their success and project a much broader scope of involvement than users of the term typically intend. A separate set of terms, building on concepts used widely during the Cold War, is shown in the second section to offer somewhat more precision, though these terms do not align closely with the PRC's own political vocabulary. The third section examines several relevant Chinese-language concepts, and suggests a basic definitional and attributional framework to accurately encompass the array of issues discussed while remaining consistent with the CCP's own understandings of its activities.

The Problem with 'Chinese Influence'

In early December 2017, as the Bennelong by-election kicked off, Australian Prime Minister Malcolm Turnbull cited 'disturbing reports about Chinese influence' in an announcement of a major shakeup of the country's national security laws.[4] Turnbull later clarified that his government was 'focused on the activities of foreign states and their agents in Australia, not the loyalties of Australians who happen to be from another country'. He also offered a tightly defined concept of 'interference', designating the line between legitimate and illegitimate foreign political activity.[5] However, it is 'Chinese influence', rather than CCP/PRC interference, that has defined the public discussion over PRC overseas political activities, as Figure 1 illustrates.

Australia appears to have led the English-speaking world in defining problems raised by PRC overseas political activities as 'Chinese influence'. Mentions of 'Chinese influence' in the far larger US media market have consistently lagged Australian media mentions of the term (Figure 2). The term has subsequently spread into UK parliamentary documents, US intelligence advice and a host of international think tank reports.[6] But it

---

[4] Tom Westbrook, 'Australia, Citing Concerns Over China, Cracks Down on Foreign Political Influence', *Reuters*, 5 December 2017.
[5] Malcolm Turnbull, 'Speech Introducing the National Security Legislation Amendment (Espionage and Foreign Interference) Bill 2017', 7 December 2017, <www.malcolmturnbull.com.au/media/speech-introducing-the-national-security-legislation-amendment-espionage-an>, accessed 22 March 2021.
[6] See House of Commons Foreign Affairs Committee, 'A Cautious Embrace: Defending Democracy in an Age of Autocracies', HC 109, Second Report of Session 2019, 4 November 2019, pp. 5, 7; US Department of Homeland Security, 'Overt Chinese Influence Targeting the Homeland', 20 February 2020,

Figure 1: Monthly Number of Articles Mentioning 'Chinese Influence' Versus 'Communist Party/CCP/PRC Interference' in Australian Media, 2017–18

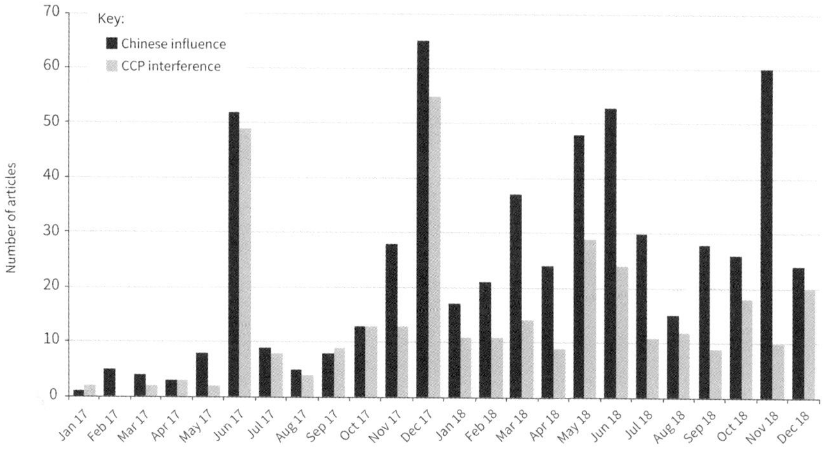

Source: Factiva search strings {Chinese influence}, {(communist party AND interference) OR PRC interference OR CCP interference) NOT chinese influence}.

projects two highly misleading conflations that carry negative consequences for both social cohesion and policymaking process.

The first is that it conflates 'Chinese' with 'PRC' or 'CCP'. While the party-state's orthodoxy holds that ethnic Chinese people are its naturally loyal allies, in fact most Chinese diaspora communities are highly diverse, including many migrants from around Southeast Asia and Greater China. Politically, overseas Chinese communities are highly diverse too, including migrants from Taiwan and Hong Kong, as well as many of the CCP's staunchest dissident opponents in exile from the mainland. As Jinghua Qian points out, 'it is people of Chinese descent who are doing most of the work of challenging Chinese authoritarianism'.[7] Far from importing authoritarian values, Chinese diaspora communities have a long and deep affinity with liberal democracy.[8] The PRC overseas

---

<www.documentcloud.org/documents/7007103-Overt-Chinese-Influence-Targeting-the-Homeland.html>, accessed 2 April 2021; Diamond and Schell (eds), 'Chinese Influence and American Interests'; Gordon Corera, 'UK Vulnerable to Chinese Influence, Report Says', *BBC*, 20 February 2019; Rob Schmitz, 'Australia and New Zealand are Ground Zero for Chinese Influence', *NPR*, 2 October 2018.

[7] Jinghua Qian, 'Call Out China's Meddling, but the Yellow-Peril Alarm at "Chinese Influence" Is Racist', *Sydney Morning Herald*, 14 September 2019.

[8] An 1878 political pamphlet produced by Chinese migrants in Melbourne illustrates well these deep roots. See L Kong Meng, Cheok Hong Cheong and

Figure 2: Yearly Number of Media Articles Mentioning 'Chinese Influence' in Australian and US Media

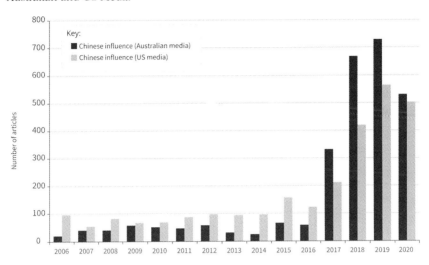

Source: Factiva search string {Chinese influence}.

political activities that have raised risks in liberal democracies are, in short, not Chinese in character.

The root of this definitional problem lies in the fact that the English-language term 'Chinese' simultaneously denotes an ethnicity, geography, culture and state. As a result, labelling problematic PRC overseas political activities as 'Chinese' projects an unwarranted association between Chinese ethnicity and the CCP's political activities.[9] Even if those who use the term are attuned to these nuances, their audiences – including politicians, bureaucrats and frontline officials and the public – may not be. Overbroad framings of policies can lead to misdirection of resources and sub-optimal outcomes.[10] For example, the US Department of Justice's 'China Initiative', launched in 2018 to curb economic espionage, has so

---

Louis Ah Mouy (eds), *The Chinese Question in Australia, 1878–1879* (Melbourne: Balliere, 1878). For a compelling longer study, see John Fitzgerald, *Big White Lie: Chinese Australians in White Australia* (Sydney: UNSW Press, 2007).
[9] Margaret K Lewis, 'Criminalizing China', *Journal of Criminal Law and Criminology* (Vol. 111, No. 1, 2021); Paul MacGregor, <twitter.com/paulmacgregorCH/status/1058574289903923201>, accessed 22 March 2021.
[10] Peter Mattis and Matt Schrader, 'America Can't Beat China's Tech Theft with Racial Profiling', *War on the Rocks*, 23 July 2019.

far produced mostly minor and unrelated charges.[11] Recent instances of non-Chinese politicians with Asian backgrounds being called 'Chinese spies' by members of the public illustrate how use of the label 'Chinese' in public policy debates over PRC political activities risks fanning racially based suspicion in the community. As detailed in Chapter III, this presents risks to social cohesion, civil liberties and national security.

A second conflation is between *influence* and *attempts* at exercising influence. As Evelyn Goh notes, influence refers to 'modifying or otherwise having an impact upon another actor's preferences or behavior in favor of one's own aims'.[12] Among the various issues discussed under the 'Chinese influence' label, the actual level of influence the PRC and its supporters have achieved ranges widely. Beijing's political red lines now powerfully shape the content of the Chinese-language news environment abroad. However, its attempts at altering the foreign and security policies of Anglophone liberal democracies have generally been abject failures, with the US, the UK and Australia all hardening their positions on key security and technology-related issues in recent years. London and Canberra's military alliances with Washington have remained a matter of bipartisan consensus, despite strongly negative public views of then US President Donald Trump during his tenure.

Failing to distinguish influence from attempts to influence is not merely a semantic problem; it carries potential negative consequences for analysis and policy. Most directly, it impedes the identification of priority areas for response.[13] Communications technology has enabled new, effective modes of PRC extra-territorial coercion against dissidents and persecuted minorities, but democracies have yet to develop any meaningful responses (see Chapter IV). Conversely, the Trump administration tightened rules on PRC propaganda outlets operating in the US, despite scant evidence that they have been successful in shaping public opinion on China.[14] As Parton observed in 2019, 'If the judgement is that certain activities are ineffective and are likely to remain so, the

---

[11] 'Asian Americans Advancing Justice, Letter to President-Elect Joe Biden on Justice Department's "China Initiative"', 5 January 2021, <advancingjustice-aajc. org/publication/letter-president-elect-joe-biden-justice-departments-china-initiative>, accessed 2 April 2021; Margaret Lewis, 'Gang Chen's Case Should Be the End of the DOJ's "China Initiative"', *SupChina*, 26 January 2021.

[12] Evelyn Goh, 'The Modes of China's Influence: Cases from Southeast Asia', *Asian Survey* (Vol. 54, No. 5, 2014), pp. 825–48.

[13] Bates Gill and Benjamin Schreer, 'Countering China's "United Front"', *Washington Quarterly* (Vol. 41, No. 2, 2018), p. 157.

[14] *The Guardian*, 'US Tightens Rules on Chinese State Media over "Propaganda" Concerns', 18 February 2020; Laura Silver, Kat Devlin and Christine Huang, 'Unfavorable Views of China Reach Historic Highs in Many Countries', Pew Research Center, 6 October 2020.

best policy is to ignore them'.[15] Finally, referring to PRC political activities as 'Chinese influence' inflates the party-state's power and masks its limitations. This too is both inaccurate and counterproductive. As the familiar idea of 'bandwagon' effects suggests (and the related Chinese concept of 'shi' [势], meaning 'momentum' or 'propensity'), the more powerful or inexorable an actor appears the more futile resistance can seem to those living in its shadow.

Cold War Redux

Another prominent set of terminology in public policy discourse on the PRC's attempts at exercising political influence abroad has revived and redeployed concepts from the early Cold War. Two of these terms – 'influence operations' and 'political warfare' – were constructed by Western analysts at the time to try to understand the overseas political activities of the Soviet Union, another Marxist-Leninist party-state, within liberal-democratic political settings. Such terms are less ambiguous than 'Chinese influence', as they generally connote the party-state rather than Chinese ethnicity as the source of problems. However, it is important to bear in mind that, despite the PRC's Marxist-Leninist character, neither of these terms is present in the CCP's own conceptual vocabulary for its political activities, which are discussed later.

Influence Operations

The concept of influence operations denotes state-coordinated political activities directed towards state goals. Unlike 'Chinese influence', this term is clearly agnostic on whether such activities succeed. A 2009 report from the RAND Corporation defines influence operations as 'coordinated, integrated, and synchronized application of national diplomatic, informational, military, economic, and other capabilities in peacetime, crisis, conflict, and postconflict to foster attitudes, behaviors, or decisions by foreign target audiences that further U.S. interests and objectives'.[16]

Competing conceptualisations exist. Another US military-affiliated source equates influence operations with psychological operations.[17] Some sources draw comparisons between PRC 'influence operations' and

---

[15] Charles Parton, 'China–UK Relations: Where to Draw the Border Between Influence and Interference?', *RUSI Occasional Papers* (February 2019), p. 1.
[16] Eric V Larson et al., *Foundations of Effective Influence Operations: A Framework for Enhancing Army Capabilities* (Santa Monica, CA: RAND Corporation, 2009), p. xii.
[17] J 'Spyke' Szeredy, 'Influence Operations: Integrated PSYOP Planning', *Air and Space Power Journal* (Vol. 19, No. 1, 2005), pp. 38–44.

the Soviet concept of 'active measures' – intelligence-led covert actions to influence events outside the USSR.[18] However, the term will be misleading unless the activities referred to are, in fact, state coordinated. It is also important to note that neither influence operations nor active measures are part of the CCP's contemporary political lexicon.

Political Warfare
Political warfare refers to state actions aimed at undermining and ultimately destroying an opponent's political system. A May 1948 US State Department memorandum outlined 'the inauguration of organized political warfare' *against* the Soviet Union, defining the concept as

> the employment of all the means at a nation's command, short of war, to achieve its national objectives. Such operations are both overt and covert. They range from such overt actions as political alliances, economic measures ... and "white" propaganda to such covert operations as clandestine support of "friendly" foreign elements, "black" psychological warfare and even encouragement of underground resistance in hostile states.[19]

This document explicitly presents political warfare as a construct for understanding the Soviet Union's zero-sum approach to politics beyond its own borders in the early Cold War prior to Nikita Khrushchev's doctrine of 'peaceful coexistence'. Its applicability to the PRC rests on the assumption that the activities in question aim at the destruction of the political system in which they occur. In Taiwan's case, this assumption holds because the PRC aims to subsume Taiwan within its polity.[20] Beyond this scope, however, the term is liable to mischaracterise the nature of the challenges the PRC's overseas political activities pose to liberal democracies.

Recent Additions: Foreign Interference and Sharp Power
The concept of 'foreign interference' has been deployed to distinguish normal foreign political activities from those that are considered

---

[18] Peter Mattis, 'Contrasting China's and Russia's Influence Operations', *War on the Rocks*, 16 January 2018.

[19] The memorandum's exact authorship is unknown, but it was drafted by the State Department's Policy Planning Staff under George Kennan. See Office of the Historian, 'Foreign Relations of the United States 1945–1950, Emergence of the Intelligence Establishment: 269. Policy Planning Staff Memorandum', 4 May 1948, <https://history.state.gov/historicaldocuments/frus1945-50Intel/d269>, accessed 2 June 2021.

[20] Mark Stokes and Russell Hsiao, *The People's Liberation Army General Political Department: Political Warfare with Chinese Characteristics* (Washington, DC: Project 2049 Institute, 2013).

unacceptable.[21] Turnbull defined foreign interference by reference to 'three Cs', namely 'covert, coercive or corrupt' activities. This was, Turnbull declared, 'the line that separates legitimate influence from unacceptable interference'. Notably, Turnbull was explicit that the term should refer to actions rather than actors: 'interference is unacceptable from any country whether you might think of it as friend, foe or ally'.[22]

The relatively precise, ideologically blind definition of 'interference' contrasts with the nebulous concept of 'sharp power'. The December 2017 report that popularised the term defined sharp power as 'authoritarian "soft power" … that pierces, penetrates, or perforates the political and information environments in the targeted countries'.[23] This description captures a wide range of legitimate or benign cultural exchange, public diplomacy and political advocacy. In contrast to interference, the distinction between acceptable soft power and 'malign' sharp power lies not in the nature of political activities in question, or their compatibility with the law or principles of liberal democracy, but in the authoritarian nature of the actor engaging in them.[24]

PRC Overseas Political Activities

Responding to the challenges presented by PRC overseas political activities requires consideration of the concepts that underpin them. Within the CCP's own policymaking systems, United Front work and Overseas Chinese work are among the most important, with specialised bureaucracies responsible for their implementation. However, an array of other concepts also inform PRC activities outside China's borders, bringing involvement from other parts of the party-state.

United Front and Overseas Chinese Work

While influence operations and political warfare are absent from the CCP's political lexicon, 'United Front' work is a Leninist concept of tactical alliances whose relevance to overseas political activities Xi himself has repeatedly emphasised. The immediate targets of the party's United Front work are individuals and groups that the CCP considers 'patriotic' but not necessarily committed ideological allies. These include intellectuals, capitalists, religious and minority ethnic groups, and more recently

---

[21] Parton, 'China–UK Relations'.
[22] Turnbull, 'Speech Introducing the National Security Legislation Amendment (Espionage and Foreign Interference) Bill 2017'.
[23] Cardenal et al., *Sharp Power*, p. 6.
[24] *Ibid.*, p. 7.

professionals and overseas students.[25] In return for aligning with the CCP's goals, these individuals and groups stand to gain prestige, connections and a degree of privileged access into the PRC political system. As Gerry Groot observes, the United Front system enables 'corporatist co-optation … of otherwise potentially dangerous elements', helping both to control and leverage such groups' knowledge, skills and connections. The CCP's fundamental ambivalence towards its United Front targets is embodied in the privileged, but arms-length, 'consultative' role granted to members of the Chinese People's Political Consultative Conference (CPPCC), the party-state's peak United Front body.[26]

The role of this CCP alliance management system has undergone several important evolutions since its inception. As a result, its current role cannot necessarily be interpreted directly through the lens of its past activities. In the 1920s and 1930s, the CCP pursued two periods of 'united front' alignment with Chiang Kai-shek's Kuomintang (KMT) against the warlords and Japanese invaders, respectively. In the Chinese Civil War after 1945, by contrast, United Front work served to isolate and subvert Chiang's regime, and is seen to have made a major contribution to the CCP's victory. After two decades of relative inactivity following the Anti-Rightist Campaign and Cultural Revolution, United Front work was reconstituted from 1978 to serve the PRC's economic construction.[27]

Today, United Front work aims at cultivating 'patriotic' links with non-party elements in the service of PRC goals. As specified in Article 2 of the CCP Central Committee's 2021 regulations on United Front work, the united front that United Front work seeks to create refers to

> the Chinese Communist Party-led, worker-peasant-based, alliance including all socialist workers, socialist entrepreneurs, patriots who defend socialism, and patriots who defend the unity of the ancestral land and strive for the great rejuvenation of the Chinese nation.[28]

Article 3 specifies the key tasks of United Front work to include 'developing the broadest patriotic united front' and supporting the realisation of 'the great rejuvenation of the Chinese nation' – implying nationalistic goals

---

[25] Kynge, Hornby and Anderlini, 'Inside China's Secret "Magic Weapon" for Worldwide Influence'; Alex Joske, 'Reorganizing the United Front Work Department: New Structures for a New Era of Diaspora and Religious Affairs Work', *China Brief* (Vol. 19, No. 9, 2019).

[26] Groot, 'United Front Work After the 19th Party Congress'.

[27] See Groot, *Managing Transitions*.

[28] Central Committee, '中国共产党统一战线工作条例' ['CCP United Front Work Regulations'], *Xinhua*, 5 January 2021, <http://www.gov.cn/zhengce/2021-01/05/content_5577289.htm>, accessed 17 March 2021. Author translation.

rather than ideological subversion, except in territories over which the PRC claims sovereignty. But Article 3 also calls for 'the maintenance of social *harmony* and *stability* and safeguarding the state's *sovereignty*, *security* and development interests'.[29] The italicised language indicates that United Front work also entails the suppression of dissent against CCP rule over territories to which it lays claim, notably Taiwan, Tibet, Xinjiang and Hong Kong.

United Front work is formally overseen by the Central Committee United Front Work Department and subordinate United Front bureaucracies at the provincial and municipal levels. However, it is formally the responsibility of every party member to cultivate non-CCP members. It has been central to the CCP's promotion of cross-straits ties and opposition to independence in Taiwan, and for its management of Hong Kong's affairs. Beyond this scope, United Front work involves promoting economic cooperation with the PRC, fomenting opposition to anti-CCP dissent, and building support for 'reunification' with Taiwan and other key PRC foreign policy positions – a function that has expanded in recent years.[30]

An overlapping party-state concept is 'Overseas Chinese' work, or the management of the PRC's relations with diaspora communities around the world. This too has domestic and international dimensions, being concerned with both the management of relations with ethnic Chinese who return to the PRC from abroad and with communities located in foreign countries. Like its predecessors, the Qing Empire and the Republic of China (ROC), the PRC has sought, via its diaspora policy, to stifle dissent and neutralise political threats from overseas Chinese communities. However, it has also long focused on the goal of drawing in overseas Chinese capital and skills for the PRC's economic development, especially since the reform era.

The effectiveness of PRC Overseas Chinese work has been greatly aided since the 1990s by the drawing down of the rival ROC Overseas Chinese work bureaucracy that accompanied 'Taiwanisation', as well as the greater receptiveness of more recent generations of émigrés to PRC political appeals.[31] The PRC's Overseas Chinese work bureaucracy was

---

[29] *Ibid*. Emphasis added.

[30] Mattis and Joske, 'The Third Magic Weapon'; Gerry Groot, 'The CCP's Grand United Front Abroad', paper presented in Prague, July 2019, pp. 7–14, <sinopsis. cz/en/the-ccps-grand-united-front-abroad>, accessed 2 June 2021; Ryan Manuel, 'The United Front Work Department and How it Plays a Part in the Gladys Liu Controversy', *ABC News*, 15 September 2019.

[31] To, *Qiaowu*, Chapters 4–5; see also Chen Jie, *The Overseas Chinese Democracy Movement: Assessing China's Only Open Political Opposition* (Cheltenham: Edward Elgar, 2019).

subsumed under the United Front Work Department in 2018, indicating the party-state leadership's desire to increase coordination and control of both internal and external United Front work.

Other PRC Concepts
Besides United Front and Overseas Chinese work, numerous other party-state concepts mandate overseas political activities. These are typically implemented by better-known bureaucracies such as the Ministry of Foreign Affairs, the Ministry of State Security (MSS) and CCP propaganda units. These include:

- 'State Security' (国家安全): China's MSS conducts overseas operations aimed at actively forestalling political threats, for instance by infiltrating and disrupting dissident organisations, and putting under surveillance key target groups such as overseas students.[32] The MSS has a 'Foreign Security and Reconnaissance Bureau' (对外保防侦察局) responsible for such tasks.[33] Communications technologies also now enable PRC police from the Ministry of Public Security (公安部) to directly intimidate overseas-based critics and ethnic minority groups, including by harassing their families in China (see Chapter II).
- 'Public Diplomacy' (公共外交), a responsibility of the Foreign Ministry that, in contrast to the English-language concept of the same name, concerns communication with audiences both inside and outside China's borders regarding foreign policy issues.[34]
- 'Foreign-Directed (External) Propaganda' (对外宣传), a narrower concept referring to mass communications directed at non-Chinese audiences, usually in non-Chinese languages.[35]
- 'International Liaison Work' (联络工作), which refers to the CCP's outreach to foreign political organisations and individuals,

---

[32] Chen, *Overseas Chinese Democracy Movement*, pp. 58–60; Nicholas Eftimiades, *Chinese Intelligence Operations* (Ilford: Frank Cass, 1994), Chapter 5, especially pp. 38–42.
[33] Peter Mattis and Matthew Brazil, *Chinese Communist Espionage: An Intelligence Primer* (Annapolis, MD: Naval Institute Press, 2019), eBook version, p. 110.
[34] Yang Jiechi, '努力开拓中国特色公共外交新局面' ['Strive to Open Up a New Situation of Public Diplomacy with Chinese Characteristics'], *Qiushi* [*Seeking Truth*] (No. 4, February 2011).
[35] Anne-Marie Brady, 'China's Foreign Propaganda Machine', *Journal of Democracy* (Vol. 26, No. 4, 2015), pp. 51–59; David Shambaugh, 'China's Propaganda System: Institutions, Processes and Efficacy', *China Journal* (No. 57, January 2007), pp. 47–50.

particularly socialist and communist parties, but also other organisations and persons, particularly those considered fraternal.[36]

- 'Military Liaison Work' (军事联络工作), the efforts of the People's Liberation Army (PLA) to engage and influence high-level counterparts in the defence and security establishments of foreign polities, especially Taiwan, through its own Political Work Department's Liaison Bureau.[37]

Many of these activities overlap with each other, and with United Front and Overseas Chinese work. This list is not exhaustive, but it illustrates the significant variety of party-state overseas political activities that exist. Each of the activities discussed so far is carried out by the party-state, but the political behaviours that they induce – if successful – may not be. This makes attribution challenging, as discussed next.

Terminology and Attribution

This paper uses 'PRC overseas political activities' – activities that influence or attempt to influence political discussions or processes outside the PRC's borders – as a descriptive umbrella term for the set of issues under discussion. This term offers five advantages. First, it is broad enough to accurately cover all the phenomena within its scope. Second, consistent with the wide array of activities included, it is a plural rather than singular term. Third, it is agnostic as to their effectiveness, leaving the scope and priority of each issue to separate processes of analysis. Fourth, it is designed to be normatively as neutral as possible. This is to facilitate rational, focused debate and deliberation on which activities constitute unacceptable foreign interference and warrant the application of state power to prevent their occurrence, which are permissible but merit political or policy responses, and which are acceptable exercises of liberal-democratic freedoms. Equating PRC overseas political activities with interference would imply a blanket ban, undermining liberal-democratic principles. And fifth, it translates easily and directly into Chinese as *haiwai zhengzhi huodong* (海外政治活动), providing basic compatibility with relevant actors' understandings of their activities.

---

[36] Christine Hackenesch and Julia Bader, 'The Struggle for Minds and Influence: The Chinese Communist Party's Global Outreach', *International Studies Quarterly* (Vol. 64, No. 3, 2020); David Shambaugh, 'China's "Quiet Diplomacy": The International Department of the Chinese Communist Party', *China: An International Journal* (Vol. 5, No. 1, March 2007), pp. 26–54.

[37] Stokes and Xiao, *The People's Liberation Army General Political Department*.

Table 1: Terminology and Attribution of Overseas Political Activities; Greyed-Out Cells Indicate Illogical or Misleading Combinations

Attribution / Political Activity Types	Influence Operations	United Front Work	Foreign Interference	Influence
Chinese: state, ethnicity, language, culture, place	Neither influence operations nor political warfare are prominent parts of the contemporary Chinese political lexicon, and contrary to civilisational framings used by some officials, cultures do not act in a sufficiently coordinated manner to justify these terms.	United Front work is a Leninist theory of tactical alliances with no particular relationship with Chinese ethnicity or culture.	Chinese communities are too diverse to be meaningfully attributed with acts of interference.	Actual effects attributable to Chinese communities or Chinese culture as a whole, none of which have been identified as problematic to liberal democracy.
Pro-PRC: citizens or supporters of the PRC or its political positions	Unless the actors concerned are directed or supported by the party-state (that is, attributable to the CCP), the activity will not be sufficiently coordinated for 'operation' to be an accurate description.	Pro-PRC political activities are a desired *result* of United Front work, but the latter is carried out by CCP cadres, party members and agents, not its targets.	Unacceptable political actions by PRC citizens or supporters.	Actual effects attributable to the citizens or supporters of the CCP.
CCP: party-state and its agents	Coordinated political activities carried out by the CCP and/or those under its direction or material support.	CCP cadres, party members and agents' activities aimed at advancing party-state interests by co-opting non-party actors.	Unacceptable political activities by the CCP and/or those under its direction or material support.	Actual effects of actions attributable to the CCP and/or those under its direction or material support.

Source: Author generated.

In a liberal democracy, individuals are held to be sovereign actors, equal under the law. Upholding this principle demands that political activities – especially problematic ones that may warrant government intervention – are accurately attributed to the actors that perform them. Foreign states are not entitled to the same rights as individuals, such that attributing an individual's actions to a foreign state may entail a diminution of that person's rights. Equitability depends on this being done only according to clearly defined standards. PRC overseas political activities may be carried out by the party-state (the CCP), or they may be spontaneous, self-directed or self-interested actions of its citizens or supporters legitimately exercising liberal-democratic freedoms. A crucial distinction must therefore be drawn between (1) the CCP and its agents, and (2) PRC citizens and pro-PRC supporters. 'Agents' refers only to people acting under the direction or material support of another.[38] The distinction is crucial because foreign states and those acting on their behalf are not entitled to the same political rights that ordinary private individuals are in a liberal democracy. They may also be justifiably subjected to more stringent disclosure requirements in the exercise of those rights to which they are entitled.

To take an illustrative example, there is a fine yet fundamentally important distinction between the CCP's United Front and Overseas Chinese work, performed by party members, cadres and agents, and the PRC-aligned words and actions of people within the target scope of United Front and Overseas Chinese work. The latter are the desired outcome of the former, but the two may or may not be causally connected. The CCP's guiding philosophy of dialectical materialism collapses this distinction, determining the character of political actions by which side of an assumed contradiction between opposing 'forces' they are perceived to fall on (see Conclusion). Liberal democracies operate from the opposite starting assumption – that political actions result from the choices of sovereign individuals pursuing their own beliefs and interests. Even if individual choices are shaped by incentive structures created by the CCP, the resulting actions cannot be attributed to the party-state without justification – such as evidence of material support or direction. Absent such evidence, actions seen to support or align with the party-state or its political positions are best described as 'pro-PRC'.[39] The key distinctions discussed above are summarised in Table 1.

---

[38] Section 11 of Australia's Foreign Influence Transparency Scheme Act 2018 defines 'on behalf of' by four criteria: '(i) under an arrangement with', '(ii) in the service of', '(iii) on the order or at the request of', or (iv) 'under the direction of'.

[39] For further discussion of the merits of various terminology, see Fitzgerald, 'Mind Your Tongue', pp. 12–18; and Anastasya Lloyd-Damnjanovic, 'A Preliminary Study

Conclusion

Concepts and terminology are crucial to the methodical and effective development of public policy, but many of the terms that now dominate the global English-language discussion of PRC overseas political activities have been vague or inaccurate. In particular, the idea of a wide-ranging, ill-defined threat to national security from 'Chinese influence' appears to have taken hold first in Australia, and then more broadly in English-language policy discourse on China. The use of such terms raises risks that range from misdiagnosed causes of problems to damage to social cohesion and even harm to national security. As the following chapter shows, liberal democracies are not in fact facing a generalised threat from 'Chinese influence'. What they are grappling with is three complex but distinct sets of risks: to national security; to civil liberties; and to academic freedom.

---

of PRC Political Influence and Interference Activities in American Higher Education', Wilson Center, 2018, pp. 33–34.

II. DISAGGREGATING THE RISKS

This chapter unpacks the array of issues the party-state and its supporters' political activities have presented to liberal democracies in Xi's 'New Era' of PRC power, highlighting significant variation in their causes, the actors involved, comparative context, and their relationship with local laws and institutions. The most basic distinctions concern three different objects of risk or threat: national security; civil liberties; and academic freedom. Some of the activities under discussion present security risks by potentially impacting the integrity of democratic systems of representation and government. However, the most directly impactful activities threaten the political rights and freedoms of particular individuals and groups, especially dissident individuals and émigré ethnic and religious groups. The third set of risks relate to the special responsibility of higher education institutions to ensure freedom of speech and intellectual enquiry for their staff, students and visitors. Various PRC overseas political activities, meanwhile, constitute normal exercises of democratic rights.

The comparative context, causes and effects of different PRC overseas political activities are also varied. In some cases, other foreign states or domestic actors conduct comparable activities, while in others the PRC's stand out as either quantitatively or qualitatively different. Significant diversity is also apparent in the causes of the risks identified. Some are straightforwardly the result of repressive policies formulated and coordinated in Beijing. Others, however, have arisen primarily from technological developments, the growth of China's economic heft, and the increasing mobility, financial means and self-confidence of PRC citizens and consumers. Finally, many of these risks are a result of shortcomings in local institutions. This is crucial for policy purposes, as it implies that the challenges raised by the PRC's overseas political activities may also represent opportunities to strengthen liberal-democratic institutions, a theme to which Chapter IV will return.

Risks to National Security

Scholars have long noted the powerful combination of linguistic openness and mobilising potential of the concept of national security.[1] Traditionally, issues of national security have been understood as those that concern the threat, or use, of violence against the state.[2] In line with a general widening of the understanding of security, the concept now commonly encompasses credible threats to the conditions of existence for the polity, such as food and water supplies, ecological environment, communication networks, and the integrity of institutions of government and electoral processes.[3] Adopting this broadened understanding, PRC overseas political activities have raised two key areas of national security risk, namely election interference and elite co-optation.[4] So far, however, their success in this area has been moderate compared with the broad-ranging encroachments on civil liberties discussed later in this chapter.

Electoral Interference

Securing elections from foreign manipulations has become a concern for democracies worldwide in the era of social media, particularly since the 2016 US presidential election, the UK's Brexit referendum the same year and the French elections in 2017.[5] In the lead-up to the 2020 US presidential election, senior officials in Trump's administration claimed, without providing evidence, that Beijing was attempting to influence the election via cyber intrusions and co-opted state and local-level leaders.[6] US intelligence

---

[1] Refining Wolfers' classic definition, David Baldwin identified the term with 'a low probability of harm to acquired values', that is, things both valued and already possessed. See Wolfers, '"National Security" as an Ambiguous Symbol'; Baldwin, 'The Concept of Security'.

[2] Edward Kolodziej, *Security and International Relations* (Cambridge: Cambridge University Press, 2005), p. 22.

[3] Barry Buzan, Ole Waever and Jaap de Wilde, *Security: A New Framework for Analysis* (Boulder, CO: Lynn Rienner, 1998); Barry Buzan and Lene Hansen, *The Evolution of International Security Studies* (Cambridge: Cambridge University Press, 2009), pp. 1–20.

[4] Other PRC-related national security risks, such as espionage, cyber security and military technology transfer, are beyond the scope of this paper.

[5] Zoe Hawkins, 'Securing Democracy in the Digital Age', Australian Strategic Policy Institute, 2017; Philip Howard, Bharath Ganesh and Dimitra Liotsiou, 'The IRA, Social Media and Political Polarization in the United States, 2012–2018', Oxford Computational Propaganda Research Project working paper, December 2018.

[6] Dustin Volz, 'U.S. National Security Adviser Says China Targeting 2020 Election', *Wall Street Journal*, 9 August 2020; Jeff Mason and Daphne Psaledakis, 'Trump Security Adviser Claims China Has Taken "Most Active Role" in Election Meddling', *Reuters*, 4 September 2020; Tom O'Connor, 'National Security Chief Says China Too Tried to Hack Election, China Said it "Doesn't Interfere"',

officers reportedly resisted attempts by Director of National Intelligence John Ratcliffe, a Trump ally, to force a stronger emphasis on China in a classified post-election report to Congress.[7] However, during the 2018 mid-term election campaigns, Beijing did engage in targeted public diplomacy against Trump's tariffs, aimed at rural Republican-voting regions.[8] This indicated that the party-state's propaganda strategists are giving close consideration to the potential electoral implications of their activities.

Anecdotal evidence from Australia also suggests that PRC authorities recognise the possibility of influencing foreign electoral voting and the political leverage it could offer. In a 2017 meeting with senior Australian Labor Party (ALP) figures, CCP security chief Meng Jianzhu allegedly suggested Beijing might discourage members of the Chinese diaspora from supporting the ALP if it did not support the bilateral extradition treaty it was seeking.[9] Contrary to Meng's reported insinuation, it is highly unlikely that overseas Chinese communities, especially citizens of foreign countries, would be manipulable as a voting bloc.[10] However, the rise of Chinese internet companies as global players has clearly created new opportunities for Beijing to influence domestic politics in overseas countries.[11]

The PRC has robust technical and institutional capabilities for influencing political content on online media platforms popular overseas such as WeChat and TikTok.[12] This creates the potential for the CCP to shape electorally relevant information circulating on such platforms. A particular source of vulnerability arises from liberal-democratic governments and political parties' use of such social media platforms as tools for public diplomacy and political campaigning.[13] In some cases, foreign politicians have had content directly censored from their PRC-

Newsweek, 22 October 2020; Daniel Funke, 'Fact-Check: Did China Orchestrate an Effort to "Overthrow Our Government and the Election"?', *Austin American-Statesman*, 19 January 2020.

[7] Jennifer Jacobs, 'Trump Spy Chief Stirs Dispute Over China Election-Meddling Views', *Bloomberg*, 16 December 2020.

[8] Josh Funk, 'Chinese Broadens its Propaganda Drive to Heartland America', *AP*, 20 October 2018.

[9] Primrose Riordan, 'China's Veiled Threat to Bill Shorten on Extradition Treaty', *The Australian,* 5 December 2017.

[10] Wanning Sun and Haiqing Yu, 'WeChat, the Federal Election, and the Danger of Insinuative Journalism', *Pearls and Irritations*, 1 February 2019.

[11] Tom Sear, Michael Jensen and Titus Chen, 'How Digital Media Blur the Border Between Australia and China', *The Conversation*, 16 November 2018.

[12] In 2019, TikTok suspended the account of a US user who posted a video discussing the PRC's mass internment of Uyghur Muslims. See Dave Lee, 'TikTok Apologises and Reinstates Banned US Teen', *BBC News*, 28 November 2019.

[13] Michael Walsh, Stephen Dziedzic and Jason Fang, 'Why are Australian Politicians Intensifying Their Presence on Chinese Social Media Platforms?', *ABC News*, 3 April

hosted social media accounts on WeChat.[14] Of equal or greater concern is the possibility that, having invested in building a following on such platforms, politicians and parties may find themselves with incentives to steer clear of political content that could result in their accounts being closed or suspended. The potential for PRC authorities to mediate the relationships between foreign politicians and their constituents in these ways threatens the integrity of democratic political systems.

Elite Co-Optation

As China's economy has boomed, the financial means and overseas interests of both the PRC party-state and Chinese enterprises have grown rapidly. At the same time, the Xi era has brought increased emphasis on political control and Leninist institutional penetration ('party-building') and co-optation of non-party actors (United Front work), increasing the necessity for enterprises and organisations to cooperate with the party-state. In these circumstances, PRC economic actors' cultivation of relationships with politicians, donations to political parties and the employment of former officials and politicians in consulting and advocacy roles have assumed sharper political dimensions. This has accentuated risks to the integrity of liberal-democratic political systems from lobbying activities by PRC or pro-Beijing actors, part of the broader issue of influence-buying in politics.

In Australia, donations to political parties from PRC-aligned business figures have generated significant concern from security agencies.[15] Senator Sam Dastyari was forced to resign from the frontbench in 2016 after donations and in-kind payments from pro-PRC tycoons appeared to influence his comments on policy issues, including a reported comment describing the South China Sea dispute as 'China's own affair'.[16] In an apparent attempt to convert such donations into policy influence, one of Dastyari's benefactors, Huang Xiangmo, reportedly threatened to

2019; Michael Walsh and Bang Xiao, '"Uncharted Territory": WeChat's New Role in Australian Public Life Raises Difficult Questions', *ABC News*, 19 April 2019.
[14] Yaqiu Wang, 'How China's Censorship Machine Crosses Borders – and Into Western Politics', Human Rights Watch, 20 February 2019.
[15] PRC citizen Huang Xiangmo headed the ACPPRC until 2017. Australian citizen Chau Chak Wing has also served in the Guangdong provincial United Front-run consultative body, the Chinese People's Political Consultative Conference. See Nick McKenzie and Richard Baker, 'Wikileaked: Billionaire Australian Donor's Beijing Links Detailed in "Sensitive" Diplomatic Cable', *Sydney Morning Herald*, 16 July 2017.
[16] Quentin McDermott, 'Sam Dastyari Defended China's Policy in South China Sea in Defiance of Labor Policy, Secret Recording Reveals', *ABC News*, 29 November 2017.

withdraw a $400,000 donation to the ALP after its defence spokesperson called for Australian naval patrols in the South China Sea in 2016.[17]

PRC companies' appointments of former politicians in lobbying roles have unsurprisingly been followed by public advocacy of policy positions preferred by Beijing on issues such as joining the Belt and Road Initiative, cooperation with PRC propaganda organs and Huawei's involvement in 5G network construction.[18] An individual's adoption of policy positions preferred by a foreign state may of course reflect sincerely held views of the national interest. Nonetheless, the provision of material benefits to people with special knowledge of, and access to, political institutions could undermine the integrity of democratic systems, especially if the arrangements are not transparently disclosed and understood by citizens.

In Australia's case, the PRC's efforts to cultivate friendly relationships with politicians have so far been considerably less effective than those of other players.[19] There is little sign of PRC-linked donations successfully influencing Canberra's security policy: its military alliance remains unquestioned by either major party in Canberra, and Dastyari hastily retracted his South China Sea remark as soon it was reported in English. This risk in Australia's case stems from broader systemic causes. The PRC accounted for almost 80% of foreign-source donations between 2000 and 2016,[20] but foreign donations make up only a small fraction of the money that Australia's major political parties accept.[21] The increasing financial means of PRC citizens and

---

[17] Gabrielle Chan, 'Sam Dastyari Contradicted South China Sea Policy a Day After Chinese Donor's Alleged Threat', *The Guardian*, 5 June 2017.

[18] Australia's former trade minister Andrew Robb took a high-paid consulting position with the PRC's Landbridge Group; ex-Foreign Minister Bob Carr was appointed by the leader of Australia's peak United Front body to head the new Australia–China Relations Institute; and former independent senator Nick Xenophon joined PRC telco Huawei after leaving parliament. See Primrose Riordan, 'Andrew Robb Under Fire for Pushing China's One Belt One Road Policy', *Australian Financial Review*, 31 October 2016; *Xinhua*, 'China-Australia Media Cooperation to Increase Cultural Understanding', *Xinhua*, 27 May 2106.

[19] Canberra was willing to stand alone with the US in rejecting a UN Human Rights Council resolution condemning the killing of dozens of Palestinians in Gaza in May 2018. See David Wroe, 'Australia Defends Voting Against "Unbalanced" United Nations Investigation into Gaza Killings', *Sydney Morning Herald*, 19 May 2018.

[20] A recent study found 79.3% of foreign donations to Australian political parties between 2000 and 2016 were from Chinese entities. See Luke Henriques Gomes, 'Nearly 80 Per Cent of Foreign Political Donations Come from China, Data Shows', *New Daily*, 12 December 2017.

[21] Joo-Cheong Tham, 'Better Regulation of All Political Finance Would Help Control Foreign Donations', *The Conversation*, 1 September 2016; Joo-Cheong Tham and Malcolm Anderson, 'Taking Xenophobia Out of the Political Donation Debate', *Inside Story*, 20 October 2016. Foreign donations were around $16 million between 2000 and 2016, but total donations have been estimated at $994

supporters have thus highlighted a general vulnerability in democratic political institutions posed by the influence of money in politics.

Risks to Civil Liberties

Whereas democratic principles require that the political system aggregates the preferences of the public as accurately as possible, liberalism holds that individuals should be free to develop and express political views of their own volition. Typically, this has entailed rights to free speech, association and assembly, as well as access to necessary information upon which to base political judgements, and equal treatment under the law. Threats to such civil rights are distinguished from national security risks by the fact that the immediate object at which the threat is directed is the individual citizen or community group, rather than the political collective as a whole. As will be seen below, in most cases, PRC threats to civil liberties fall disproportionately on diaspora groups, and the impact within these communities has often been severe.

Extra-Territorial Suppression of Dissent

The CCP has attempted to stifle overseas critics using coercive techniques throughout its period of rule, and especially since the violent crackdown on student-led protests in 1989. Well-documented methods include threatening members of the target's family in China, denial of visas to critics seeking to visit their families and intimidation through conspicuous surveillance.[22] Beijing has also signalled that anti-CCP activities or speech outside China can entail permanent exile by detaining numerous prominent overseas diaspora critics who have set foot in the PRC. The case of Swedish-Chinese bookseller Gui Minhai, seized from Hong Kong in 2016, and the arrest of Chinese-born academic Yang Hengjun, held since January 2019 and recently charged with vague offences against state security, project strong threats of punishment for political activities conducted outside the PRC's borders.[23]

---

million over approximately the same period. See Democracy for Sale, 'Reported Donations to Reach $1 Billion in 2015-16', 7 December 2016.

[22] Kelsey Munro, 'Australian Critic of Beijing Refused Entry to China', *The Guardian*, 22 March 2018. According to unconfirmed, anonymous US intelligence information, several PRC citizens in Australia have been kidnapped and transported to China. See Zach Dorfman, 'The Disappeared', *Foreign Policy*, 29 March 2018; Suzanne Smith, 'Chinese Spying on Dissidents Reaches New Levels', *Crikey*, 8 October 2019.

[23] Hannah Beech, 'China's Search for Dissidents Has Now Expanded to Foreign Countries', *TIME*, 18 January 2016; Ben Doherty, 'Yang Hengjun: Australian Writer

Modern communications technologies, such as instant messaging and video calling, have created new possibilities for extra-territorial political coercion. A PRC student in Australia received video calls from police in China who were with her family, ordering her to desist from political activism including mocking Xi on Twitter and participating in rallies in support of Hong Kong's protest movement. At one point an officer explicitly told the student 'although you are [in Australia], you are still governed by the law of China'.[24] Similarly, Uyghurs and other ethnic groups have faced technology-enabled surveillance and intimidation by PRC security services after fleeing repressive policies.[25]

The PRC's success in interfering with the exercise of political rights that are nominally protected in liberal democracies reflects a general institutional shortcoming in liberal democracies with multicultural societies. Members of other diaspora communities have faced similar encroachments from authoritarian regimes, including Ethiopia, Saudi Arabia, Cambodia and Rwanda, which have all attempted to suppress critics abroad, sometimes using brute force, in recent years.[26] Russia is suspected of targeting dissidents in the UK and elsewhere with extreme

---

Held in China for Almost Two Years Officially Charged with Espionage', *The Guardian*, 10 October 2020.

[24] Lin Evlin, 'This Activist Says She is Being Tracked and Harassed in Australia by Chinese Police', *SBS News*, 12 July 2020. The activist, who uses the English pseudonym 'Zoo', described the harassment of her family over her activities in Australia in a video. See DongWuyuan Zoo, <https://twitter.com/Horror_Zoo/status/1268353070666092547>, 02.25, 4 June 2020, accessed 18 March 2021.

[25] Megha Rajagopalan, 'They Thought They'd Left the Surveillance State Behind. They Were Wrong', *BuzzFeed*, 9 July 2018; Andrew Beattie, 'China's Police State Goes Global, Leaving Xinjiang Refugees in Fear', *Arab News*, 23 July 2019, <https://www.arabnews.com/node/1529551/world>, accessed 18 March 2021.

[26] Ethiopian and Rwandan government critics have seen family members arrested over their participation in protests on Australian soil, and Cambodian dissidents have complained of threats and surveillance by agents or supporters of Hun Sen's government. Further afield, Vietnamese agents abducted a businessman in Berlin in 2017, sparking fears among dissident exiles that have reverberated in Vietnamese communities elsewhere. See Human Rights Watch, 'Australia: Protests Prompt Ethiopia Reprisals', 7 November 2016; Amy Greenbank, 'Refugees Living in Fear as Alleged Foreign Spy Network Infiltrates Australian Suburbs', *ABC News*, 25 August 2019; Stephen Dziedzic, 'Hun Sen: Calls for Cambodian Sanctions Intensify in Canberra Ahead of Key Julie Bishop Meeting', *ABC News*, 15 August 2018; Silke Ballweg, 'Berlin Bloggers Fear the Long Arm of Hanoi', *DW*, 15 January 2018; Madeline Chambers, 'Germany Charges Vietnamese Man in Ex-Oil Executive Kidnapping', *Reuters*, 7 March 2018; before Taiwan's democratisation, the ruling Kuomintang (KMT) also engaged in intimidation and violence against its critics overseas, including the infamous murder of KMT critic Henry Liu in California in 1984. See Mark Arax, 'Rooted in Taiwan Connection: The Plot to Kill Henry Liu – Slayers Confess Details', *Los Angeles Times*, 3 March 1985.

measures, as in the poisoning of defectors Sergei and Yulia Skripal in 2018 and a number of unexplained deaths of émigrés.[27] The PRC's activities are greater in scope than those of smaller and less capable states, and quite possibly have more impact on the right to free speech of diaspora communities than other states. However, preventing such extra-territorial encroachments on minority groups' civil liberties is evidently a more general policy challenge for liberal democracies.

Control of Chinese-Language Media Platforms
In recent decades, overseas-based Chinese-language media have become much less willing to criticise the party-state or cover topics Beijing considers politically sensitive than they once were.[28] PRC propaganda organs have developed a 'borrowed boat' method whereby they channel propaganda content through established overseas media outlets by entering into partnerships with local traditional and online media entrepreneurs.[29] In the Xi era, PRC security agencies have intensified their existing efforts to pressure local businesses to withdraw advertising from overseas Chinese media outlets that criticise CCP policy.[30] In many traditional media markets, the only alternative to PRC propaganda is the *Epoch Times*, which is aligned with the Falun Gong religious organisation and, more recently, far-right causes.[31] The Chinese-language traditional media landscapes have consequently suffered from a deficit of independent content.

The rise of social media platforms as news delivery mechanisms has exacerbated these issues by enabling direct and indirect PRC censorship of

---

[27] Intelligence and Security Committee of Parliament, *Russia*, pp. 17–18; Lucy Pasha-Robinson, 'The Long History of Russian Deaths in the UK Under Mysterious Circumstances', *The Independent*, 6 March 2018.

[28] Wanning Sun, 'Chinese-Language Media in Australia: Development, Challenges and Opportunities', Australia–China Relations Institute, 2016, p. 25.

[29] Koh Gui Qing and John Shiffman, 'Voice of China: Beijing's Covert Radio Network Airs China-Friendly News Across Washington, and the World', *Reuters*, 2 November 2015; a particularly nefarious example is the co-production of film content, which has resulted in CCP propaganda being presented as documentary films. See David Bandurski, 'Documenting China's Influence', in Ivan Franceschini and Nicholas Loubere (eds), *Dog Days: A Year of Chinese Labour, Civil Society, and Rights, Made in China Yearbook 2018* (Canberra: ANU Press, 2019).

[30] Chen, *The Overseas Chinese Democracy Movement*, pp. 72–73. For a first-hand account, see Graeme Smith and Louisa Lim, 'Control and Capture: Taming Overseas Chinese Media', *Little Red Podcast* (No. 3, 2 November 2017), <http://ciw.anu.edu.au/news-and-media/media/control-and-capture-taming-overseas-chinese-media>, accessed 22 March 2021.

[31] Hagar Cohen and Echo Hui, 'The Power of Falun Gong, Part 3', Background Briefing, *ABC*, 9 August 2020.

overseas media content. Authorities in Beijing have the capability to compel censorship over the PRC-based social media platforms, notably WeChat, that many overseas Chinese media depend upon for content distribution. More routinely, Beijing's policies require proactive censorship by the companies that run the platforms, such as WeChat's owner Tencent, and Weibo's parent company Sina.[32] In turn, news organisations using such platforms may feel a need to steer clear of certain subjects, views and individuals, lest their account with valuable audiences of followers – be suspended.

Several interacting factors have brought about this abrogation of the rights of Chinese-speaking communities to reliable political information. The PRC's propaganda, state security, United Front and Overseas Chinese work bureaucracies have established a powerful combination of 'carrots' and 'sticks' that shape the political information supply of diaspora Chinese speakers. A second factor is audience preferences: many Mandarin-speaking recent arrivals from the PRC may be more accustomed to jingoistic 'red' nationalism than critiques of the CCP.[33] A third is the relative lack of funding available for credible, independent local journalism in Chinese language, commensurate with the size of overseas Chinese communities.[34] Recognising this confluence of causes has important implications for the development of policy options to address this encroachment on the rights of Chinese-speaking communities, as detailed in Chapter IV.

Co-Optation of Community Organisations

The CCP United Front Work Department, fronted by the China Council for the Promotion of the Peaceful National Reunification (中国和平统一促进

---

[32] Wang, 'How China's Censorship Machine Crosses Borders'; Tom Blackwell, 'Censored by a Chinese Tech Giant? Canadians Using WeChat App Say They're Being Blocked', *National Post*, 4 December 2019; Alex Hern, 'Revealed: How TikTok Censors Videos That Do Not Please Beijing', *The Guardian*, 25 September 2019; see also Sam Biddle, Paulo Victor Ribeiro and Tatiana Dias, 'Invisible Censorship: TikTok Told Moderators to Suppress Posts by "Ugly" People and the Poor to Attract New Users', *The Intercept*, 16 March 2020.

[33] According to one expert on overseas Chinese media, some popular online outlets self-censor controversial topics and opinions to avoid offending their audiences' pro-PRC patriotic sensibilities. Author interview with Chinese media expert, WeChat, December 2018.

[34] Qing and Shiffman, 'Voice of China'. In Australia, in addition, the removal of statutory limits on foreign ownership of Australian media outlets in 2007 has paved the way for the CCP's advances into Australian Chinese-language media. See Keri Phillips, 'The History of Media Regulation in Australia', *ABC Radio*, 6 October 2015.

会) and its 90-plus regional subordinate associations (CPPRCs) worldwide, has become increasingly visible in asserting pro-PRC political positions overseas, particularly in the Xi era.[35] They serve simultaneously as umbrellas designed to 'unify' local overseas Chinese community groups and as platforms for lobbying. The two roles complement each other. As umbrella organisations, they offer smaller local Chinese community groups the opportunity to become affiliates, which can provide the smaller groups' members with an entry point into business and social networks inside and outside China, and the PRC's diplomatic outposts and the United Front and Overseas Chinese work systems within China. As platforms, they claim to represent 'the' Chinese community in voicing pro-PRC positions on issues of importance to Beijing, while cultivating ties with political elites and building goodwill towards the party through philanthropy.

Recent years have brought a proliferation of local United Front-aligned groups claiming to represent a vast array of religious, hometown and professional sub-groups within Chinese diaspora communities.[36] Australia's CPPRC listed 81 branches and affiliated member groups as of late 2017, and more than 150 groups signed on to its statement denouncing Hong Kong's protest movement in 2019.[37] The UK's peak

---

[35] The Chinese-language names of these regional or country-level peak United Front bodies typically follow the pattern '[country/region]-Council of the Promotion of the Peaceful Reunification of China ([所在国/地名]中国和平统一促进会)', though their local-language names can vary widely. John Dotson, 'The United Front Work Department in Action Abroad: A Profile of the Council for the Promotion of the Peaceful Reunification of China', *China Brief*, 13 February 2018; John Dotson, 'The United Front Work Department Goes Global: The Worldwide Expansion of the Council for the Promotion of the Peaceful Reunification of China', *China Brief* (Vol. 18, No. 2, 2019).

[36] Graeme Smith, Louisa Lim and Gerry Groot, 'How to Make Friends and Influence People: Inside the Magic Weapon of the United Front', *Little Red Podcast*, 9 April 2018, 9–13 mins, <omny.fm/shows/the-little-red-podcast/how-to-make-friends-and-influence-people-inside-th>, accessed 22 March 2021.

[37] The list of 81 affiliated organisations was circulated at the 2017 annual members' convention held on 25 November 2017. See AUST333, 'ACPPRC 2017 Members' Convention 澳洲和统会2017会员大会', 澳中文网', 26 November 2017, <webcache.googleusercontent.com/search?q=cache:0aOBVBBOJYgJ:fj.52hrtt.com/web/news_info.do%3Fid%3DC1511403742812+&cd=1&hl=en&ct=clnk&gl=uk>, accessed 22 August 2019; this is no longer available, but an archived copy is available from the author. For the August 2019 ACPPRC-led joint statement denouncing Hong Kong protest activities and 'foreign forces interfering in Hong Kong affairs', see 'Australian Chinese Community Groups' Joint Statement on the Present Hong Kong Situation 澳大利亚华人社团对当前香港事态的联合声明', *Australian News Net*, 15 August 2019, <www.1688.com.au/breaking_news/2019/08/15/634516>, accessed 22 March 2021.

CPPRC body (全英華人華僑中國統一促進會), known in English as the 'UK Promotion of China Re-Unification Society', brought out 113 groups as co-signatories to a 2016 pro-PRC statement on Hong Kong.[38] Meanwhile, some long-established independent Chinese community associations, such as the Chinese Benevolent Society of Vancouver, have come under the control of pro-Beijing leaderships, often through democratic internal processes.[39]

Freedom of association is a basic right in a liberal democracy, although others' rights to information may require that affiliations with foreign states is publicly disclosed. The complexity of the PRC's United Front organisational system can present challenges in this regard. The CCPPRC is officially a 'United Front work system unit' (统战系统单位), so its subordinate country-level CPPRCs can be understood unambiguously as United Front organisations.[40] However, their dozens or even hundreds of member organisations may be a step further removed, as affiliates of a CCP front organisation, rather than CCP front organisations themselves. Indeed, many continue to serve as mutual-assistance societies for Chinese migrants, providing vital social support functions and business opportunities to members who may lack opportunities and skills to operate in the mainstream of the host society. Where the party-state is involved in setting up such organisations, however, the right to political information mandates that this be publicly declared.

The success of Beijing's efforts to secure political alignment from Chinese community organisations is not simply a function of United Front and Overseas Chinese work, and their intensification under Xi. But like the successful co-optation of diaspora media platforms, there are other important factors at play. First, it is also a result of the PRC's increased economic size, which has boosted overseas Chinese

---

[38] UK Promotion of China Re-Unification Society (UKPCRS), 'UKPCRS Statement of Support for the National People's Congress Interpretation of the Hong Kong Basic Law 全英华人华侨中国统一促进会关于支持全国人大对香港基本法解释的声明', 7 November 2016, <www.ukpcrs.com/documents?lightbox=i0wa7>, accessed 22 March 2021.

[39] Interviewees described an entirely democratic takeover of one venerable Australian Chinese institution. Author interviews with academic experts on Chinese community organisations, July 2018. The 124-year-old Chinese Benevolent Association of Canada (加拿大溫哥華中華會館) has led a series of high-profile collective pro-PRC statements on political issues since 2014. Tom Blackwell, 'Vancouver Group Runs Newspaper Ad Praising Controversial New Security Law in Hong Kong', *National Post*, 18 July 2020.

[40] Central United Front Work Department Propaganda Office, '中国统一战线新闻网 [China United Front News Network]', undated, <tyzx.people.cn/GB/372195/383921/384711>, accessed 13 October 2020 via Archive.org, <https://web.archive.org/web/20150509225632/http://tyzx.people.cn/GB/372195/383921/384711/>.

Table 2: Types of United Front Organisations

Organisations	Relationship to PRC Party-State
CCP Central United Front Work Department (中共中央统一战线工作部)	CCP party centre
China Council for the Promotion of Peaceful National Reunification (中国和平统一促进会)	CCP United Front work system unit
(Regional Country) Councils for the Promotion of the Peaceful Reunification of China (地区/地方) (中国和平统一促进会)	CCP overseas United Front organisations
Local member groups and affiliates of regional or country CPPRCs: hometown, professional, trade, religious, etc. community groups	United Front-affiliated organisations

Source: Author generated. Author translations.

businesses' motivations to operate in Mainland China. Another less widely understood factor is how the CCP's efforts have been helped by the withering of the ROC's Overseas Chinese bureaucracy after 'Taiwanisation', which has prompted many formerly pro-ROC overseas groups to turn to the PRC for support.[41] Finally, like the changing audience profile for overseas Chinese media content discussed above, it also reflects newer migrants' use for, and in some cases economic dependence on, United Front-aligned associations to access the commercial benefits of connections with local CCP authorities in China.[42]

The possibility that community organisations' pro-CCP political positions reflect pragmatic, material considerations rather than ideological commitment has important policy implications. As noted in Chapter I, the co-optation strategy behind the CCP's United Front work is premised on an assumption that the 'patriotic' groups targeted are not inherently loyal to the CCP – indeed, the recognition that target groups pursue their own interests rather than automatically following the CCP is what creates the need for United Front work in the first place. This suggests that host-country governments may have opportunities to expand their own relationships with these and other groups.

Many governments and political parties leverage their overseas diaspora as sources of economic and political support. India's ruling Bharatiya Janata Party (BJP) has a diaspora diplomacy policy that seeks to make overseas Indians 'be India's voice even while being loyal citizens

---

[41] To, *Qiaowu*, p. 105.
[42] Manuel, 'The United Front Work Department and How it Plays a Part in the Gladys Liu Controversy'.

in those countries'.[43] Australia's latest Foreign Policy White Paper, too, declared that Canberra would 'continue to leverage the knowledge, networks and expertise of our expatriates through chambers of commerce and organizations'.[44] However, it is unlikely that any other state can match the resources and organisational experience of the PRC's overseas agencies. The possibility of the PRC party-state using its vast organisational and financial resources to set up new United Front-affiliated associations risks crowding out independent community organisations, making political representation more difficult for diaspora communities. Suppressing organisations for taking pro-PRC political positions would violate basic principles of freedom of association, but democratic governments need to ensure channels of community representation are not dominated by PRC-aligned groups to the exclusion of other sections of the Chinese community.

Political Direct Action
PRC supporters, both organised and spontaneous, have taken public direct actions in support of the PRC government's positions on various issues in recent years. Typical examples have included mobilisations to neutralise protests by Tibetan activists and Falun Gong supporters during diplomatic visits by CCP leaders; demonstrations against unfavourable international developments such as the international arbitration ruling on the South China Sea issue in July 2016; and counter-protests against pro-Hong Kong activism in 2019. In some cases, PRC supporters have mobilised direct action to prevent public events on issues they consider offensive.[45] A prominent UK case took place at Durham University in 2018, where overseas PRC students complained to the Chinese embassy about a debating society event featuring a speaker supportive of Falun Gong. The embassy then phoned the debating society to express its 'serious concerns' and warned the event could harm UK–China ties.[46] The debate went ahead as planned.

These types of political mobilisations result from both general and specific factors. On one hand, China's consular authorities have in recent years become more willing to encourage the expression of patriotic

---

[43] Rama Lakshmi, 'Narendra Modi Urges the Indian Diaspora to Become an Extension of Foreign Policy', *The Guardian*, 2 May 2015.
[44] Australian Government, 'Foreign Policy White Paper: Opportunity Security Strength', Department of Foreign Affairs and Trade, November 2017, pp. 112–13.
[45] Ben Child, 'Melbourne Film Festival Site Crashed by Chinese Protesters', *The Guardian*, 3 August 2009; for US examples, including an attempt to pressure UCSD to rescind its invitation to the Dalai Lama to deliver a graduation day address, see Lloyd-Damnjanovic, 'A Preliminary Study', pp. 85–88.
[46] Jim Waterson, 'The Chinese Embassy Told Durham University's Debating Society Not to Let This Former Miss World Contestant Speak at a Debate', *Buzzfeed*, 10 February 2017.

sentiments among citizens and supporters overseas. After pro-PRC counter-protesters disrupted a pro-Hong Kong rally at the University of Queensland in 2019, for example, the local PRC consulate-general praised the action as 'patriotic'.[47] On the other hand, PRC citizens are increasingly wealthy, mobile, politically aware and confident to express their political views on controversial issues.[48] Finally, new technologies have created innovative forms of political coercion. This can include the obtrusive filming of public events, which can intimidate targets by implicitly communicating threats of punishment by foreign authorities.[49]

Several key variations are apparent in the relationship of such direct political action with the PRC party-state, and their implications for the democratic rights of others. Most fundamentally, while some have been largely spontaneous mobilisations, others have received sponsorship or direction from party-state authorities. Second, while many demonstrations have sought legitimately to voice pro-PRC viewpoints, others have been geared towards suppressing other viewpoints. In 2019, for example, controversies erupted on university campuses in the UK and several other countries over 'Lennon Walls' – large arrays of coloured Post-it notes carrying thoughts from supporters of the Hong Kong protest movement. In some cases, the Lennon Walls were torn down or vandalised, while in others they prompted respectful and productive dialogue.

Overseas supporters of many foreign governments – including authoritarian regimes – exercise the core democratic right of political expression through protest and public speech.[50] Two key questions, however, define the relationship of such mobilisations with liberal-democratic values:

1. Is the activity carried out on the behalf of a foreign state?
2. Does the activity interfere with the expression of others' political viewpoints?

---

[47] Xu Keyue, 'Chinese Consulate in Australia Praises Patriotic Students for Counter-Protest Against Separatists', *Global Times*, 25 July 2019, <https://www.globaltimes.cn/content/1159212.shtml>, accessed 2 April 2021.

[48] Although not necessarily increasingly nationalistic judging by the comparatively small size of recent demonstrations compared to the mass anti-foreign movements against the US in 1999, Japan in 2005, and France in 2008. Survey data casts further doubt on the common assumption that nationalism is 'rising' in China. See Alastair Iain Johnston, 'Is Chinese Nationalism Rising? Evidence from Beijing', *International Security* (Vol. 41, No. 3, 2017), pp. 7–43.

[49] Gerry Shih and Emily Rauhala, 'Angry Over Campus Speech by Uighur Activist, Chinese Students in Canada Contact Their Consulate, Film Presentation', *Washington Post*, 14 February 2019.

[50] Lloyd-Damnjanovic, 'A Preliminary Study', pp.13–14.

Table 3: Four Types of Political Mobilisation

	Spontaneous	**State-Directed**
Expressive	Not sponsored or directed by foreign state and does not interfere with others' expression of political views.	Sponsored or directed by a foreign state but does not interfere with others' expression of political views.
Suppressive	Interferes with others' expression of political views, but not sponsored or directed by a foreign state.	Interferes with others' expression of political views, sponsored or directed by a foreign state.

Source: Author generated.

These two fundamental distinctions generate four fundamentally different types of mobilisation. The first, *expressive spontaneous* mobilisations, present no threat to democratic freedoms. In fact, these are exercises of core freedoms in a liberal democracy. The second, *expressive state-directed* actions, may threaten the public's right to political information if the state's role is obscured from view. The third, *suppressive spontaneous* protest, may place others' rights to free expression at risk, so civil intervention may be required to ensure others can exercise their rights. The fourth, *suppressive state-directed* actions, constitute state-directed violation of the political rights of other people, and thus merit serious penalties. It is important that governments and universities take account of these differences in formulating appropriate policy responses aimed at better upholding political freedoms in their countries and on their campuses.

Paid Propaganda
In a striking contrast with the cash-starved media landscape in many liberal democracies, CCP English-language propaganda outlets have received large injections of funds since 2009. Some estimates run as high as $10 billion.[51] In this context, numerous media organisations have signed cooperation and content-sharing agreements with CCP propaganda organs. Most commonly this has resulted in the insertion of multi-page colour advertorial supplements about China provided by CCP propaganda organs.[52] In 2018 the PRC attempted to mobilise US domestic opposition to the Trump administration's trade war using this channel.[53]

---

[51] Shaun Mantesso and Christina Zhou, 'China's Multi-Billion Dollar Media Campaign "A Major Threat for Democracies" Around the World', *ABC News*, 7 February 2019.
[52] Bao Jie, 'Media Cooperation Highlights China-Australia Ties', *People's Daily Online*, 28 May 2016.
[53] Funk, 'Chinese Broadens its Propaganda Drive'.

Liberal-democratic societies are defined by tolerance of opposing political viewpoints. There is so far little evidence that income streams from propaganda inserts have influenced regular English-language coverage, where both professional imperatives and market incentives favour negative coverage. In Australia, Fairfax Media, owned by Nine Entertainment Co., has taken a strong critical line on many PRC-related issues in recent years (see Chapter III), despite running *China Daily* inserts until December 2020.[54] In the UK, there are signs that the coronavirus pandemic has prompted media outlets to reconsider their deals with PRC propaganda organs.[55] However, it is possible that they may produce dependencies that influence coverage in the future. This forms part of a broader issue regarding the media's editorial independence in relation to commercial interests that has worsened as media organisations' traditional revenue streams have dried up in the internet era.

Agreements enabling liberal media organisations access to the PRC news and information market are potentially more threatening to the public's right to reliable political information. Such agreements are likely to be tacitly or explicitly conditional on self-censorship by media organisations. There is evidence of actual influence being exerted in this way. For example, after signing an agreement with the Shanghai Media Group in 2014, the Australian Broadcasting Corporation (ABC) launched a website aimed at PRC audiences that avoided sensitive political topics such as the 4 June 1989 massacre in Beijing. In a dark irony, the agreement had been signed on the 25th anniversary of that violent crackdown.[56] As with many of the issues already discussed, the risks to civil liberties from such agreements fall disproportionately on those of diaspora groups: PRC authorities have tended to be more censorious towards Chinese-language content than that in English or other languages.

Inducement of Self-Censorship
The PRC has stepped up pressure on public and private institutions to modify their language to align with orthodox CCP views of Taiwan and

---

[54] Amanda Meade, 'Nine Entertainment Newspapers Quit Carrying China Watch Supplement', *The Guardian*, 8 December 2020; Glenn Dyer, 'Fairfax Running Chinese Communist Party Propaganda', *Crikey*, 17 February 2017; Myriam Robin and Glenn Dyer, 'Some Propaganda with Your Morning Paper? Why Fairfax is Spruiking for Putin', *Crikey*, 18 September 2014.
[55] Jim Waterson and Dean Sterling Jones, 'Daily Telegraph Stops Publishing Section Paid for by China', *The Guardian*, 14 April 2020.
[56] Paul Barry, 'ABC and the Great Firewall of China', *Media Watch*, 9 May 2016; Australian Broadcasting Corporation, 'ABC and Shanghai Media Group Sign International Agreement', *ABC News*, 4 June 2014.

other issues, and to avoid activities related to political subjects. In 2018, PRC state agencies issued a series of demands for companies with commercial interests in the party to modify errant website nomenclature. In one case, consular officials persuaded a local council in Queensland to erase an ROC flag painted by a local school pupil from a piece of public artwork.[57] Such pressure may have had a deterrent effect on the institutions in question, or on other institutions. In 2017–18 the Royal Court Theatre in London suspended a play on life in contemporary Tibet following advice from the British Council that it could jeopardise the theatre's ability to operate in China and cooperate with PRC artists.[58] In 2019 and 2020 several Australian venues backed away from hosting academic and artistic events on issues deemed 'sensitive' by Beijing, and a Canadian pride parade disinvited Hong Kong activists.[59]

The actual success rate of such PRC attempts at exerting political pressure is difficult to measure; successful cases are non-events, so the evidence may be hard to observe. But the documentary record is decidedly mixed. Numerous PRC campaigns have failed spectacularly, drawing major negative publicity.[60] Others have raised major additional attention and sympathy for the critics the PRC or its supporters sought to silence.[61] Yet there is little doubt that the increased economic heft of the PRC and its increasingly mobile citizens has increased the material incentives for foreign actors to comply with – or even anticipate – Beijing's demands for limits on speech. As with many of the issues discussed above, this poses a disproportionate risk to the free speech rights of the Greater Chinese diaspora, especially PRC political dissidents, ethnic minorities, and those from Taiwan, Hong Kong and Xinjiang.

---

[57] Amber Hooker, 'Why We Painted Over Students' Taiwan Flag: Council Explain', *Morning Bulletin*, 10 May 2018.

[58] Ben Quinn, 'Royal Court Dropped Tibet Play After Advice from British Council', *The Guardian*, 4 April 2018.

[59] Steph Harmon, 'Australian Gallery Accused of Censoring Democracy Activists Over Hong Kong Event', *The Guardian*, 27 August 2019; Claire Loewen, 'Hong Kong Activists Booted From Montreal Pride Parade After Alleged Pro-Communist Threats', *CBC*, 27 August 2019.

[60] In mid-2018, for example, the PRC embassy demanded the Australian *60 Minutes* programme cancel a report on its military activities in the Pacific Islands – but rather than complying, journalists penned a series of follow-up articles recounting the PRC diplomats' crude attempts at exporting censorship. Charles Woolley, '"Take This Down": Embassy's Fury Over 60 Minutes' Chinese Mega-Wharf Investigation', *9 News*, 18 June 2018.

[61] A PRC campaign against the Melbourne Film Festival's screening of a documentary on Uyghur activist Rebiya Kadeer introduced the previously unknown Uyghur leader's profile among Australians. Ben Child, 'Rebiya Kadeer Row Engulfs Melbourne Film Festival', *The Guardian*, 15 July 2009.

Risks to Academic Freedom

As designated venues for advanced research and teaching, higher education institutions in many countries are legally obliged to take steps to ensure that freedom of unfettered intellectual enquiry is upheld and protected.[62] Internationally recognised norms mandate that such institutions enable 'an atmosphere of academic freedom'.[63] Exact definitions of academic freedom vary, but generally entail the institutional autonomy from external political and economic influences, and the rights of staff, students and visitors to intellectual enquiry and expression, including on controversial issues, matters of public policy and the institution itself.[64] PRC overseas political activities have raised several challenges to upholding these tenets. Most are rooted in

---

[62] See 'Education (No. 2) Act 1986 (UK)', section 43; 'Higher Education Standards Framework (Threshold Standards) 2015 (Australia)', section 6.1(4).

[63] The 1997 UNESCO 'Recommendation Concerning the Status of Higher-Education Teaching Personnel' affirmed that the provision of education is a state obligation, that 'the right to education, teaching and research can only be enjoyed in an atmosphere of academic freedom', and that universities have an obligation to 'ensur[e] that students are treated fairly and justly, and without discrimination'. The concept had earlier been explicitly associated with European and American academic traditions, as codified in collective statements such as the American Association of University Professors' 1940 'Statement of Principles on Academic Freedom and Tenure' and the Rectors of European Universities' 1988 'La Magna Charta delle Università Europee'. However, the latter has now been signed by universities in 88 countries, including five in the PRC. See UNESCO, 'Recommendation Concerning the Status of Higher-Education Teaching Personnel', Adopted by the General Conference at its twenty-ninth session, Paris, 11 November 1997, <http://portal.unesco.org/en/ev.php-URL_ID=13144&URL_DO=DO_TOPIC&URL_SECTION=201.html>, accessed 2 April 2021; American Association of University Professors, '1940 Statement of Principles on Academic Freedom and Tenure', undated, <https://www.aaup.org/report/1940-statement-principles-academic-freedom-and-tenure>, accessed 2 April 2021; 'Signatory Universities', Observatory Magna Chartum Universitatum, undated, <www.magna-charta.org/magna-charta-universitatum/signatory-universities>, accessed 22 March 2021.

[64] Former Australian High Court justice Robert French has proposed a seven-point definition of academic freedom that distinguishes it from regular concepts of freedom of speech by reference to institutional autonomy and additional freedoms to research (staff), intellectual enquiry (staff, students), express opinions on the institution (staff, students), make public comment (staff), and participate in academic bodies (staff) and student societies (students). Robert French, 'Report of the Independent Review of Freedom of Speech in Australian Higher Education Providers', Australian Government, March 2019, pp. 230–31; see also John Fitzgerald, 'Academic Freedom and the Contemporary University: Lessons From China', *Journal of the Australian Academy of the Humanities* (No. 8, 2017), pp. 8–22; and Katharine Gelber, 'As Melbourne University Staff Strike over Academic Freedom, It's Time to Take the Issue Seriously', *The Conversation*, 8 May 2018.

the marketisation of university economics, the rise of the PRC as a market for overseas education, and failures by institutions to put in place appropriate safeguards for academic freedom in those circumstances. As with the risks to political rights discussed above, the impact falls disproportionately on minority groups within the staff and student populations.

Financial Dependencies
In the UK and Australia, cuts to public funding and the reorganisation of higher education on a profit-seeking basis have increased institutions' dependence on markets for education. The growth of the PRC's market has both accelerated and accentuated this existing challenge to the institutional autonomy upon which academic freedom depends. This has created incentives to seek and maintain connections with the PRC party-state in order to secure market access and compete with other overseas academic institutions. However, such links also create potential vulnerability to political pressure from the party-state, as well as incentives to proactively avoid controversy, for example by not hosting events on campus that would cross the party's known 'red lines', such as Tibet, Xinjiang and Taiwan. In the UK there is anecdotal evidence of university administrators responding to pressure from the PRC embassy to stifle discussions on such topics.[65] Higher-education providers reliant on the PRC market are understandably concerned about the possibility of boycotts if their institution becomes embroiled in a controversy over the PRC's long list of 'sensitive' issues.[66]

A related risk is that institutions may fail to provide sufficient support to staff to enable free intellectual enquiry and expression on subjects considered controversial by Beijing. Some universities have appeared to show less than unequivocal support for their faculty following demands from PRC students for alterations to teaching materials. In August 2017, for example, a Sydney University IT lecturer felt compelled to issue a statement of apology after using a world map that depicted PRC-claimed disputed territory as part of India. In another example, PRC student complaints over a business lecturer's references to Taiwan as a 'country' prompted a Newcastle University (Australia) statement calling for staff and students to respect cultural sensitivities.[67]

---

[65] Foreign Affairs Committee, 'A Cautious Embrace', p. 6.
[66] Author telephone interview with university administrator, December 2017.
[67] Gwyneth Ho, 'Why Australian Universities Have Upset Chinese Students', *BBC News*, 5 September 2017; Andrea Booth, 'Chinese Students Left Fuming After Sydney Uni Lecturer Uses Contested Map of China-India Border', *SBS News*, 22 August 2017. For a range of comparable examples in the US, see Lloyd-Damnjanovic, 'A Preliminary Study', pp. 79–84.

In August 2020, the University of New South Wales' social media channels deleted tweets of an article critical of China's Hong Kong policies, following protests from PRC students, prompting the vice chancellor to apologise for removing the tweets and reaffirm commitment to academic freedom.[68] The mere perception that an institution may not be fully committed to academic freedom can generate incentives for academic self-censorship.[69]

It is crucial to recognise that PRC students are not the source of the risk to academic freedom. Students are entitled to hold illiberal views and make demands for curbs on others' free speech; such demands do not themselves violate rights of free expression or academic freedom, and in fact, they are exercises of them. Nor are PRC students unique in advancing illiberal political positions or seeking to silence others on campus with whom they disagree; well-documented examples include pro-Armenian students disrupting speakers accused of denying the Armenian genocide, and supporters of the Israeli state seeking to punish academics involved in the Boycott, Divest, Sanctions (BDS) movement.[70] Indeed, campus politics in liberal democracies, like public discourse in general, has shown a trend towards narrowing the bounds of acceptable speech.[71] It is the institutions' responses to such demands that determine whether academic freedom is upheld or sacrificed in the pursuit of education markets.

Punitive and Coercive Disclosures of Campus Speech

Like many authoritarian states,[72] PRC authorities have long sought to monitor political activities of Chinese students overseas, particularly since

---

[68] Ian Jacobs, 'Statement on Freedom of Speech', University of New South Wales, 10 August 2020.

[69] A 2018 survey that asked China scholars what support they received from their institutions in dealing with the Chinese government found 'none' to be the most common response. Sheena Greitens and Rory Truex, 'Repressive Experiences Among China Scholars: New Evidence from Survey Data', *China Quarterly*, online (2019), p. 20. See also Lloyd-Damnjanovic, 'A Preliminary Study', p. 65.

[70] Jewish Voice for Peace, 'Stifling Dissent: How Israel's Defenders Use False Charges of Anti-Semitism to Limit the Debate over Israel on Campus', 2015; Lloyd-Damnjanovic, 'A Preliminary Study', pp. 13, 84–85, 87–88.

[71] French, 'Report of the Independent Review'. This comparative context has been overlooked in some analyses of PRC overseas political activities. See, for example, Thorsten Benner et al., 'Authoritarian Advance: Responding to China's Growing Political Influence in Europe', GPPi/MERICS, 2018, p. 32.

[72] Layla Quran, 'Saudi Students in U.S. Say Their Government Watches Their Every Move', *PBS NewsHour*, 19 March 2019; the CCP's one-time rival, the KMT was once particularly energetic in sending party members to report on dissent at universities

the 1989 Tiananmen protest movement.[73] It is unclear how wide-ranging the CCP's channels of political reporting on overseas students are today, but there is sufficient evidence to confirm that the practice does occur.[74] In some cases this potential for disclosure has been openly leveraged as intimidation, with participants in pro-PRC demonstrations threatening to report opponents to PRC authorities.[75] The much-scrutinised Chinese Students and Scholars Associations (CSSA), PRC embassy-affiliated campus social and pastoral groups, may have been involved in monitoring and reporting dissent. However, the CSSA's relationships with the party-state, and degree of politicisation, vary significantly from branch to branch – and within branches across time, depending on the individuals involved.[76] Temporary CCP branches have also been established abroad to monitor and control groups of exchange students at overseas universities.[77]

Contact between overseas students and their embassies and consulates is normal and often necessary. But the possibility of channels of reporting from university classrooms to authoritarian state authorities undermines academic freedom by creating implicit threats of punishment for the expression of specific political viewpoints. Mainland Chinese students are by no means the only student group targeted overseas by authoritarian governments.[78] However, they may face higher levels of

---

overseas. See, for example, Chen, *The Overseas Chinese Democracy Movement*, p. 173; and To, *Qiaowu*.

[73] Lloyd-Damnjanovic, 'A Preliminary Study', pp. 16–19.

[74] Linda Jakobson and Bates Gill, 'Is There a Problem with Chinese International Students?', *China Matters*, 21 September 2017, p. 3; Fran Martin, 'How Chinese Students Exercise Free Speech Abroad', *The Economist*, 11 June 2018; Bethany Allen-Ebrahimian, 'China's Long Arm Reaches Into American Campuses', *Foreign Policy*, 7 March 2018.

[75] Human Rights Watch, 'China: Government Threats to Academic Freedom Abroad', 21 March 2019; Scholars at Risk, 'Obstacles to Excellence: Academic Freedom and China's Quest for World-Class Universities', 2019, p. 86.

[76] While some are politically strident and closely connected with PRC embassies and consulates, others have little official contact and no engagement in politics. In the wake of the 1989 crackdown and well into the 1990s, dissident students managed to take control of many CSSAs. Chen, *The Overseas Chinese Democracy Movement*, p. 68; author interview with Australian academic, Perth, July 2018. For a case in which CSSA was demonstrably involved in reporting student speech, see MCI vs. Jie Yong Qu, Federal Court of Appeal of Canada, 2001 FCA 399, 21 December 2001, <decisions.fca-caf.gc.ca/fca-caf/decisions/en/item/31509/index. do>, accessed 2 April 2021.

[77] Bethany Allen-Ebrahimian and Alex Joske, 'The Chinese Communist Party Is Setting Up Cells at Universities Across America', *Foreign Policy*, 18 April 2018.

[78] John Heathershaw, 'Dictators Beyond Borders? Authoritarian Challenges to the Integrity of Professional Services, the Protection of Refugees, and Academic

risk due to the PRC party-state's organisational capabilities and increased emphasis on political work targeting overseas students since 2017.[79] Academic institutions have provided a permissive institutional environment for such coercion, termed here 'punitive disclosure', through a lack of appropriate student support services or explicit prohibitions on such practices (see Chapter IV).

Institutional Entanglement

Beijing offers selected foreign universities significant resources for Mandarin Chinese language learning through its Confucius Institutes (CIs). Hosting a CI also offers universities potential advantages in competing for the PRC education market; as one former CI director described it, they can work 'like a business card for all sorts of connections in China'.[80] In return, the universities provide the institutional prestige and platform for the PRC to pursue its objective of promoting 'cultural soft power'. CIs have generally been established as joint ventures between universities and the Office of the Leading Group for the International Promotion of Chinese Language. The office, commonly known as Hanban, is part of the Ministry of Education, which sits within the party-state's propaganda and ideological work system.[81] In June 2020, the PRC moved responsibility for managing the CI programme to a newly formed charitable foundation named the Chinese International Education Foundation.[82]

Freedom in the UK', written evidence to House of Commons Foreign Affairs Committee, 23 July 2019, <http://data.parliament.uk/WrittenEvidence/ CommitteeEvidence.svc/EvidenceDocument/Foreign-Affairs/Autocracies-and-UK-Foreign-Policy/Written/105181.html>, accessed 2 April 2021; Ayeshagul Nur Ibrahim, 'Oral Evidence to House of Commons Foreign Affairs Committee', 5 June 2019, <http://data.parliament.uk/writtenevidence/committeeevidence.svc/ evidencedocument/foreign-affairs-committee/autocracies-and-uk-foreign-policy/ oral/102827.pdf>, accessed 2 April 2021; Saipira Furstenberg et al., 'The Internationalization of Universities and the Repression of Academic Freedom', *Freedom House*, 2020. In addition, the author's colleagues at Lancaster University indicated concerns about similar channels of reporting to the government of Saudi Arabia; private communication with university academic, 11 January 2021.

[79] United Front Work Department Research Office, 'Ningxin juli kaichuang tongyi zhanxian shiye xin jumian' ['Gather Minds and Power to Create a New Situation for the United Front Enterprise'], *Qiushi* [*Seeking Truth*] (No. 19, 2017).

[80] Author interview with academic expert on Chinese politics, Perth, July 2018.

[81] Hanban, 'About Us', Office for Chinese Language Council, undated, <english. hanban.org/node_7719.htm>, accessed 22 March 2021 via Archive.org; Shambaugh, 'China's Propaganda System', p. 30.

[82] Confucius Institute U.S. Center, 'Clarity Around Hanban Name Change', undated, <www.ciuscenter.org/clarity-around-name-change>, accessed 22 March 2021.

In their language and cultural promotion activities, CIs – and the Confucius Classrooms they offer to local schools – can deliver tangible benefits to communities where opportunities to learn Mandarin are lacking. One long-term student at a CI in Australia has noted how in his local area, 'if you want to learn a language it is extremely difficult to find a class for any language anywhere with sufficient numbers to go ahead. If the Confucius Institute was not there it would just be another activity that we could not participate in'.[83] Even so, however, evidence of CIs' effectiveness in shaping communities' views of the PRC is mixed. One study estimated the tone of media coverage of China warmed by an average of 6% in areas where CIs were present. But surveys of US school students attending Confucius Classrooms found no pro-China effect on their views.[84]

CIs' institutional integration into universities – one difference between CIs and comparable initiatives from other states, such as the Japan Foundation, Goethe-Institut and British Council – raises two distinct risks to academic freedom. One is the possibility, discussed above, that the benefits they confer on universities could become a source of leverage, or an incentive to self-censorship.[85] Most CIs have steered clear of politics, though there have been scattered instances of censorious behaviour of junior and senior Hanban officials.[86] However, the PRC's increasing internal repression and external confidence also suggest political use of CIs as leverage might grow in future.[87]

---

[83] Published at Jason Gallaher, 'Feedback From a Confucius Institute Student', China Matters, 23 May 2018, <https://chinamatters.org.au/wp-content/uploads/2018/05/Jason-Gallaher_Confucius-Institute-Response_052018.pdf>, accessed 2 April 2021.

[84] Samuel Brazys and Alexander Dukalskis, 'Rising Powers and Grassroots Image Management: Confucius Institutes and China in the Media', *Chinese Journal of International Politics* (Vol. 12, No. 4, 2019), pp. 557–84; Naima Green-Riley, 'The State Department Labeled China's Confucius Programs a Bad Influence on U.S. Students. What's the Story?', *Washington Post*, 25 August 2020.

[85] Jackson Kwok, 'Is There A Problem with ... Confucius Institutes?', *China Matters Policy Brief*, May 2018.

[86] In the most internationally infamous incident, the current Hanban Director-General Xu Lin once ordered pages to be torn from the programme booklet for the European Association of Chinese Studies conference in Braga, Portugal. A number of more quotidian examples of censoriousness can be found in Rachelle Peterson, *Outsourced to China: Confucius Institutes and Soft Power in American Education* (New York, NY: National Association of Scholars, April 2017).

[87] As Jackson Kwok has noted, CI directors have been asked to promote high-level PRC policies such as the Belt and Road Initiative. Kwok, 'Is There A Problem with ... Confucius Institutes?'.

A second source of risk lies in the content of some of the formal contractual arrangements that establish CIs. While many CIs have operated with a high degree of autonomy from Beijing, some contracts assigned Hanban a degree of authority over academic matters such as teaching assessment,[88] and few have allowed for faculty oversight or review of CI activities.[89] Academic freedom may be particularly challenged where CIs are involved in for-credit teaching of China studies topics beyond language and culture, given the institutional constraints they operate within on the PRC side. The specific arrangements of CIs varies across locales, and their foundational agreements have generally not been publicly available, making the risks difficult to assess. The impact on contractual arrangements of the recent institutional shift on the PRC side, from Hanban to the Chinese International Education Foundation, also remains to be seen.

Self-Censorship
Academic self-censorship – alterations to research agendas or presentations due to political considerations – can occur on an organisational or individual level. On the organisational level, publishers that carry academics' work have shown some susceptibility to the kinds of political pressures the PRC has brought to bear on other companies with commercial interests in China (as discussed above). For example, in 2017 academic and commercial publishers, including Springer Nature and Cambridge University Press (CUP), complied with PRC government orders to censor content for users in China. While CUP eventually reversed its decision following an international outcry, Springer Nature's decision remains in place.[90]

On the individual level, there are a wide range of family, research and ethical reasons why individual academics – and indeed think tank researchers, commentators and journalists – may choose to avoid sensitive topics or soften public criticism of Beijing.[91] Two European academics reportedly refused to publish an article in an academic journal

---

[88] Fergus Hunter, 'Universities Must Accept China's Directives on Confucius Institutes, Contracts Reveal', *The Age*, 25 July 2019.
[89] Kwok, 'Is There A Problem with … Confucius Institutes?'; Hunter, 'Universities Must Accept China's Directives'; author telephone interview with US academic, December 2018.
[90] Marv Kennedy and Tom Phillips, 'Cambridge University Press Backs Down Over China Censorship,' *The Guardian*, 21 August 2017.
[91] For a thorough discussion of these self-censorship issues based on interviews with faculty at US universities, see Lloyd-Damnjanovic, 'A Preliminary Study', pp. 62–75.

alongside a paper they regarded as too controversial.[92] In a 2018 survey of China researchers, more than 15% said they had decided against pursuing a research project due to its sensitivity, and 24% said they had adjusted a project's focus, in many cases in consideration of the safety of others. In total, 70% of respondents agreed that 'self-censorship is a problem in the China field'.[93]

The PRC's efforts to control discussion inside and outside China are the proximate cause of self-censorship, but a lack of institutional support mechanisms is an important enabling factor. The above mentioned survey of China scholars found nearly 10% had been interviewed by PRC police about their research, and around 5% had experienced trouble obtaining visas over the preceding decade. But the survey also found 'none' to be the most common response regarding the support they received from their institutions in dealing with the Chinese government.[94] Researchers with family in the PRC can face major additional risks to exercising normal academic freedoms that neither universities nor liberal-democratic governments have so far attempted to mitigate.

Conclusion

This chapter has sought to disaggregate the diverse risks that PRC overseas political activities have presented to liberal democracies. Risks to national security are distinct from threats to civil liberties, and it is in the latter category that the PRC's activities appear to have made the greatest impact. These can be understood as risks of *inaction* in response to the political activities of an empowered PRC and its supporters. Chapter III will turn to the risks of reaction, with a focus on Australia's experience with public policy based on aggregated treatment of issues through a national security lens.

---

[92] Phila Siu, 'What's the "Dirty Secret" of Western Academics Who Self-Censor Work on China?', *South China Morning Post*, 21 April 2018.
[93] Greitens and Truex, 'Repressive Experiences Among China Scholars'.
[94] *Ibid.*, p. 20.

III. RISKS OF REACTION: AUSTRALIA'S EXPERIENCE WITH AGGREGATION

Chapter II illustrated the varied risks that overseas political activities of the CCP and its supporters have presented to liberal democracies, particularly those with multicultural societies. These can be understood as the risks of inaction. But the risks of responding to these challenges also demand careful consideration. Australia offers an example of public policy responses based on the aggregation approach that addresses this array of issues primarily as a matter of national security. This may have helped to mobilise rapid legislative action and rally other liberal democracies to action. However, as this chapter argues, Australia's experience also illustrates major drawbacks to the aggregation-based approach.

Canberra's efforts to counter PRC political activities have been hailed – and promoted – internationally as a pioneering model to follow.[1] In February 2018, then US Assistant Secretary of Defense Randy Schriver said Australia had 'done us a great service by publicising much of this activity and then taking action'.[2] National Endowment for Democracy Vice President Christopher Walker testified to a US Congressional hearing that European states should 'learn from countries, such as Australia, that

---

[1] Amy Searight, 'Countering China's Influence Operations: Lessons from Australia', Center for Strategic and International Studies, 8 May 2020; Daniel Tobin, 'How Xi Jinping's "New Era" Should Have Ended U.S. Debate on Beijing's Ambitions', Testimony Before the U.S.-China Economic and Security Review Commission, Hearing on 'A "China Model?" Beijing's Promotion of Alternative Global Norms and Standards', 13 March 2020, p. 14; John Garnaut, 'How China Interferes in Australia', *Foreign Affairs*, 18 March 2018; Euan Graham, 'The Pitfalls of Pragmatism in Australian Strategic Policy', *ASPI Strategist*, 27 February 2020; Diamond and Schell, 'Chinese Influence and American Interests', p. 147.

[2] Peter Hartcher, 'Australia Has "Woken Up" the World on China's Influence: US Official', *Sydney Morning Herald*, 27 February 2018.

are farther along on the learning curve in dealing with China's sharp power'.[3] The UK and Singapore's foreign ministries have flagged intent to study Australia's legislative response as they formulate their own policies to counter PRC interference.[4] Yet besides the PRC propaganda organs' shrill denunciations of Australia's responses as 'racist' and 'paranoid', they have so far not been subjected to focused critical scrutiny outside the country.

On close inspection, Australia's response has left some of the most impactful PRC activities unaddressed, and it remains unclear if the legislated expansions in the power of national security agencies have warranted the associated diminishments in civil liberties. This chapter focuses on three interrelated problems in Australia's aggregative response. First, drawing together diverse issues into a wide-ranging national security threat produced a highly charged public discourse that has at times veered into alarmism and ethnic profiling. This has helped the CCP appeal to the loyalties of ethnic Chinese in Australia and fanned xenophobia in the community, harming social cohesion and ultimately national security. Second, legislation rushed through parliament during this period of agitated public discourse has been less effective in countering PRC political interference than expected, while carrying significant costs to civil liberties. Third, national security agencies have become increasingly involved in the provision of public policy information and the protection of diaspora communities' civil liberties, tasks for which such agencies are not typically well suited.

Alarmist Public Discourse

Australian journalists have shed important light on many of the issues discussed in the preceding chapter.[5] However, presentations in the Australian media have often elided important distinctions between different issues, rolling them together into an amorphous story of pervasive infiltration. Headlines and commentaries have presented a wide array of PRC and pro-Beijing activities as a coordinated 'operation' (often labelled 'Chinese') involving an assortment of spies, propagandists,

---

[3] Christopher Walker, Testimony Before the U.S.-China Economic and Security Review Commission Hearing on 'China's Relations with U.S. Allies and Partners in Europe and the Asia Pacific', 5 April 2018, p. 4.
[4] House of Commons Foreign Affairs Committee, 'A Cautious Embrace', p. 9; Nick Bonyhady, 'Australia's Anti-Foreign Interference Laws a Model for Singapore', *Sydney Morning Herald*, 5 March 2019.
[5] For a brief review of the Australian media's reporting, see Kelsey Munro, 'A Free Press is a Magic Weapon Against China's Influence Peddling', *Lowy Interpreter*, 18 December 2017.

community groups, businesspeople, academics and students systematically subverting Australia's sovereignty and political system.[6]

An agenda-setting 2017 TV segment aired on *Four Corners*, ABC's flagship investigative programme, exemplified the presentation of an array of genuine issues within a national security frame. It opened with a dramatic re-enactment of a midnight raid on the home of an Australian ex-intelligence analyst – married to a politically connected PRC woman convicted of bribery in the US – suspected of illegally removing classified information. The security breach was then woven together with issues ranging from political co-optation to coercion of dissidents, control of Chinese-language media and campus activities of overseas Chinese student groups, forming an elaborate narrative of widespread, insidious 'power and influence'. Shadowy lighting and tension-laden sound effects reinforced the espionage theme throughout the 45-minute programme.[7] An extensive accompanying feature published by Fairfax Media was headlined *China's Operation Australia*, presenting a further expanded array of activities as a coordinated state 'operation'.[8]

After these high-profile exposés, public commentators and politicians have elaborated widely on the themes of pervasive 'Chinese' infiltration and subversion of Australian government, society and institutions. While many have attempted to train the focus on CCP interference rather than Chinese communities as the sources of threat, the aggregation of issues – especially under imprecise labels such as 'Chinese influence' – has placed Chinese-Australians under broad-based suspicion. The result has been damage to social cohesion and the fanning of xenophobia in politics and the wider community.[9]

---

[6] For a catalogue of alarmist headlines, see James Laurenceson, 'Do the Claims Stack Up? Australia Talks China', Australia-China Relations Institute, 29 October 2018. For a similar compendium for the US, see Eric Fish, 'Hostile Rhetoric Toward Chinese International Students: A Compilation', *Medium*, 21 October 2019, <https://ericfish85-47480.medium.com/negative-rhetoric-about-chinese-international-students-a-compilation-b6cf45128c9f>, accessed 22 March 2021.

[7] Nick McKenzie, 'Power and Influence', *Four Corners*, 5 June 2017; a sequel aired in September 2019 framed a set of China-related issues at universities, ranging from unethical research collaborations that could contribute to repression and genocide in Xinjiang, to duelling student protests over Hong Kong, as the 'infiltration of Australia's universities by the Chinese Communist Party'. See Sean Rubinsztein-Dunlop, 'Red Flags', *Four Corners*, 14 October 2019.

[8] Nick McKenzie et al., 'China's Operation Australia: The Party Line', *Sydney Morning Herald*, June 2017.

[9] Osmond Chiu, 'I Was Born in Australia. Why Do I Need to Renounce the Chinese Communist Party?', *Sydney Morning Herald*, 14 October 2020; Adam Ni and Yun Jiang, 'Submission to the Select Committee on Foreign Interference via Social Media', 12 March 2020, p. 3.

Overgeneralised and Ethnically-Based Suspicions

Leading Australian commentators have presented the PRC migrant population in general as a threat to the country's values and interests. Former defence official Paul Dibb wrote in 2016 that a 'considerable number of Chinese residents and students' constitute 'a group of people who are not integrating and who owe allegiance to a foreign power'.[10] In his influential polemic, *Silent Invasion: China's Influence in Australia*, academic Clive Hamilton repeatedly questioned the 'loyalty' of hundreds of thousands of Australian residents with PRC backgrounds.[11] While disavowing any ethnically-based discrimination, prominent author and political editor Peter Hartcher argued that reductions in migration from the PRC (in favour of Hong Kong and Taiwan) were necessary in order to exclude 'phony Australians who are here to serve the interests of a foreign autocracy bent on bleeding Australia's sovereignty'. Hartcher went on to argue that Chinese-Australians 'need help' in upholding 'loyalty to Australia and its people'.[12]

Many Australian commentators, particularly China specialists, have attempted to draw clear distinctions between the PRC's political activities and Chinese ethnicity. Others have been less careful. In *Silent Invasion*, Hamilton repeatedly links Chinese ethnicity with various kinds of espionage,[13] and he subsequently stated that the CCP had 'poisoned the well' of potential Chinese-Australian political candidates.[14] Australian Values Alliance president Feng Chongyi has argued the 'majority of Chinese Australians' are pro-CCP nationalists with only a wavering commitment to Australia, who are willing to turn out in their hundreds of thousands 'to wave the red flag'.[15]

The notion of 'Chinese' infiltration has gained traction with far-right nationalists in Australia and beyond. When US ethno-nationalist Steve Bannon granted his first Australian media interview in July 2018, several MPs in Canberra endorsed his analysis that the country was situated in an existential 'fight for the ages' on behalf of 'Western tradition' against Chinese control. One of the MPs, Andrew Hastie, who then chaired the Parliamentary Joint Committee on Intelligence and Security, also echoed

---

[10] Paul Dibb, 'China Allegiance Fuels Concern', *The Australian*, 6 September 2016.
[11] Hamilton, *Silent Invasion*, pp. 4–5, 281. Hamilton estimates that only 'around twenty to thirty per cent [of Chinese-Australians] are loyal to Australia first'. The issue of loyalty appears on at least 35 of the book's 281 pages.
[12] Peter Hartcher, 'Response to Correspondence', *Quarterly Essay* (No. 77, 2020).
[13] Hamilton, *Silent Invasion*, pp. 161, 162, 165, 170, 172, 173, 176.
[14] Jamie Tarabay, 'Australia's Toughest Question: How Close Is Too Close to China?', *New York Times*, 19 September 2019.
[15] Quoted in Peter Hartcher, 'Red Flag: Waking Up to China's Challenge', *Quarterly Essay* (No. 76, 2019), p. 63.

FBI Director Christopher Wray's description of China as a 'whole-of-society threat'.[16] Hastie had earlier chosen to highlight businessman Chau Chak Wing's ethnicity in an extraordinary speech delivered under parliamentary privilege, in which he referred to the pro-CCP property developer as a 'Chinese-Australian citizen' linked to a UN bribery case.[17] At an October 2020 parliamentary hearing, Chinese-Australian witnesses were repeatedly challenged by senators to 'unconditionally condemn the Chinese Communist Party dictatorship', a position the Australian government itself is unwilling to take.[18] No non-ethnically Chinese witnesses to the inquiry were requested to make similar statements.

Public discourse that has the effect of casting generalised suspicions towards large groups such as PRC-born migrants or ethnic Chinese is detrimental to both civil liberties and national security. It furthers the CCP's United Front work objective of appealing to the Chinese diaspora, especially recent arrivals, and bolsters its propaganda lines that attempt to conflate 'Chineseness' with identification with the party-state. At the same time, it is likely to damage relations between governments and Chinese diaspora communities at a time when national security agencies increasingly depend upon such relationships in their attempts to counter the threats the PRC poses.[19] It also runs counter to basic liberal values.[20]

Fuelling Racism
The surge of alarmist public policy discourse from 2017 quickly put pressure on Chinese-Australian communities. The regular appearance of anti-Chinese slogans in public underscored the risk of overheated public discourse fanning anti-Chinese nationalism in the community, and a 2020 survey of Chinese-Australians found nearly 20% reported being

---

[16] Peter Hartcher, 'Australia on the Front Line of Clash with China, Says Steve Bannon', *Sydney Morning Herald*, 9 July 2018.

[17] *Hansard (Australian Parliament)*, 'Appropriation (Parliamentary Departments) Bill (No. 1) 2018–2019, Second Reading', House of Representatives, 22 May 2018, pp. 110–12.

[18] *Hansard (Australian Parliament)*, 'Issues Facing Diaspora Communities in Australia', Senate Foreign Affairs, Defence and Trade References Committee, 14 October 2020, pp. 4–6.

[19] Lewis, 'Address to the Lowy Institute'; Australian Government, 'Australia's Counter Foreign Interference Strategy'; Ni and Jiang, 'Submission to the Select Committee on Foreign Interference via Social Media', p. 3.

[20] As Wanning Sun has pointed out, 'to distrust your own citizens and question the allegiance of PRC migrants on the basis of the actions of a few individuals [is] taking a crucial step towards undermining the "brand" of Australia as a liberal democracy'. See Wanning Sun, 'Correspondence: *Red Flag*', *Quarterly Essay*, undated, <www.quarterlyessay.com.au/correspondence/all>, accessed 17 March 2021.

'physically threatened or attacked' over their background in the preceding 12 months.[21] In Australia, narratives of Chinese infiltration and takeover quickly spread in populist political circles. Senator Pauline Hanson, who made worldwide headlines in the 1990s with her warnings that Australia was being 'swamped by Asians', said in a 2019 TV interview, 'I believe that they've got their eyes on Australia … they're slowly taking it … not by stealth but by cunning'.[22] A far-right colleague of Hanson's warned in the Senate that Beijing had 'influence over some, many possibly, Chinese in this country'.[23] The website of the openly racist fringe party Australia First ran a series of articles categorised under campaign themes of 'Chinese Invasion of Australia' and 'Outlaw and Deport Chinese Migrants'.[24]

Alarmist political discourse also damages social cohesion by discouraging participation in politics among already underrepresented diaspora communities.[25] Following headlines about 'Chinese Manchurian candidates' during the Bennelong by-election in 2017, one Chinese-Australian local politician told the *New York Times* he felt he needed to avoid being photographed with particular members of the diaspora in order to avoid suspicion.[26] In 2020, Chinese-Australian politicians in New South Wales received letters threatening death to 'all Chinese people'.[27]

---

[21] Natasha Kassam and Jennifer Hsu, 'Being Chinese in Australia', Lowy Institute, March 2021. At multiple university campuses in Melbourne posters written in poorly formed Chinese characters declared 'Attention: no Chinese allowed in here'. At Sydney University, a swastika and the words 'kill Chinese' were scrawled prominently on a toilet wall. See Josh Butler, 'Racist Graffiti Splashed Across Sydney University', *Ten Daily*, 4 July 2018; Tyrone, '"No Chinese Allowed" Signs Seen Around Universities in Melbourne', *Crossing the Wall* (blog), 24 July 2018; Heidi Han, '"Kill Chinese" and Nazi Symbol Found Scrawled on Sydney Uni Grounds', *SBS*, 3 August 2017.

[22] Richard Ferguson, 'Hanson: China "Would Love Their Hands on Australia"', *The Australian*, 5 August 2019.

[23] Kirsten Lawson, 'Crossbench Unites on China Threat', *Canberra Times*, 3 December 2019.

[24] As of March 2020, there were 140 articles in the 'Chinese Invasion of Australia' category, <australiafirstparty.net/category/globalist-enemies/chinese-invasion-of-australia>, accessed 22 March 2021.

[25] This was a common theme in parliamentary testimonies from Chinese-Australians in *Hansard (Australian Parliament)*, 'Issues Facing Diaspora Communities in Australia'; see also Yun Jiang and Adam Ni, 'Confronting Foreign Interference in Australia', *The Diplomat* (No. 63, February 2020).

[26] Damien Cave, 'Espionage Bills in Australia Stir Fears of Anti-Chinese Backlash', *New York Times*, 19 December 2017; Jieh-yung Lo, 'Just Because I Have a Moderate View on China Doesn't Make Me a Beijing Stooge', *The Guardian*, 5 April 2018; Fitzgerald, 'Mind Your Tongue', p.10.

[27] Naaman Zhou, 'Death Threats, Distrust and Racism: How Anti-Chinese Sentiment "Seeped Into the Mainstream"', *The Guardian*, 3 March 2021.

Chinese-Australian politicians accused of links to United Front-affiliated community and business groups have been subjected to both legitimate scrutiny and unfounded 'spying' innuendo.[28] A candidate in a 2018 local election had campaign materials daubed with racist graffiti after a politician in the Tasmanian state parliament publicly linked her candidacy with 'evidence that the Chinese government is seeking to influence the outcome of Hobart City Council elections'.[29] Even citizens from non-Chinese backgrounds have been targeted: Liberal Party councillor Elizabeth Lee, who is Korean-Australian, said in September 2020 that she had received online abuse labelling her a 'Chinese spy'.[30]

In a testimony to an Australian Senate inquiry into issues facing diaspora communities in October 2020, former Australian public servant Yun Jiang described a 'toxic environment' facing Chinese-Australians seeking to participate in public life:

> many Chinese-Australians are choosing to remain silent and refusing to speak out publicly on Australia's foreign and domestic policies. On the one hand, if they criticise the Chinese government, then their family may face trouble, or they may have difficulties going to China in the future. They may also be accused of being a race traitor by a Chinese nationalist. On the other hand, if they criticise

---

[28] In December 2018, when Western Australia state MP Pierre Yang was revealed to have been a member of two Australian CPPRC-affiliated community groups, media headlines sensationally claimed he had once 'served aboard' a Chinese 'spy ship'. It was in fact the Australian Defence Force that sent Yang to serve on the PRC ship. See Andrew Burrell, 'WA Labor MP Pierre Yang Served Aboard Suspected China Spy Ship', *The Australian*, 6 December 2018; Liberal MP Gladys Liu was justifiably scrutinised over her involvement in pro-PRC organisations and fundraising activities, but far-right pundits then also demanded she denounce China's militarisation in the South China Sea and declare Xi a dictator. Such demands would not normally be made of a backbencher with no expertise or responsibility for such policy areas. See Qian, 'Call Out China's Meddling, but the Yellow-Peril Alarm at "Chinese Influence" Is Racist'. Clive Hamilton even suggested Liu, an Australian citizen born in British Hong Kong, might owe 'allegiance' to a foreign power, requiring her removal from parliament. See Clive Hamilton, 'Why Gladys Liu Must Answer to Parliament About Alleged Links to Chinese Government', *The Conversation*, 11 September 2019.
[29] The Greens leader, Cassie O'Connor, read a series of quotes from candidate Yongbei Tang before declaring the existence of the evidence of Chinese government attempts to influence the election. See Cassie O'Connor, 'Foreign Influence in Local Government Elections', Tasmanian Greens, 27 September 2018; *ABC Radio Hobart*, 'Tasmanian Greens Leader Doubles Down on Chinese Election "Meddling" as Slurs Hit Candidate', 15 October 2018.
[30] Tom Lowrey, 'Liberal and Labor Canberra Politicians Tell of "Hurtful" Racism on the ACT Election Campaign Trail', *ABC News*, 25 September 2020.

the Australian government, they're suspected of being an agent for foreign interference, having their loyalties questioned or accused of being brainwashed. This is a toxic environment for Chinese-Australians to be in.[31]

Expansion of National Security

Six months after the ABC's *Power and Influence* and Fairfax's *China's Operation Australia* catapulted PRC overseas political activities into Australia's national consciousness, the Turnbull government launched a wide-ranging legislative response it said was designed to counter 'unprecedented and increasingly sophisticated attempts to influence the political process'.[32] The package included:

- Electoral Legislation Amendment (Electoral Funding and Disclosure Reform) Act, passed in December 2018, banning foreign donations to political parties (hereafter 'EFDR Law').
- Foreign Influence Transparency Scheme Act, passed in June 2018, establishing a new public registry for policy advocacy on behalf of foreign principals ('FITS Law').
- National Security Legislation Amendment (Espionage and Foreign Interference) Act, also passed in June 2018, expanding the scope of espionage and secrecy offences, and introducing new criminal penalties for covert, deceptive or coercive interventions into political processes ('EFI Law').[33]

This sweeping suite of legislation mirrored the aggregated handling of PRC overseas political activities in Australia's public discourse on the subject. Indeed, proponents of the laws have credited the ABC and Fairfax media presentations as their impetus, and described how further media investigations had been necessary to 'regain control of the conversation' and secure their passage in the face of opposition from various sectors of Australian society.[34] Figure 3 corroborates these accounts, illustrating the close relationship between the Australian

---

[31] *Hansard (Australian Parliament)*, 'Issues Facing Diaspora Communities in Australia', p. 1.

[32] Henry Belot, 'Malcolm Turnbull Announces Biggest Overhaul of Espionage, Intelligence Laws in Decades', *ABC News*, 5 December 2017.

[33] The originally tabled bills were: 'Electoral Legislation Amendment (Electoral Funding and Disclosure Reform) Bill 2017 (Australia)'; 'Foreign Influence Transparency Scheme Bill 2017'; 'National Security Legislation Amendment (Espionage and Foreign Interference) Bill 2017'. The finally enacted versions are referred to below as 'EFDR Law', 'FITS Law' and 'EFI Law', respectively.

Figure 3: Australian Media Discussion of 'Chinese Influence' and Australia's Legislative Response

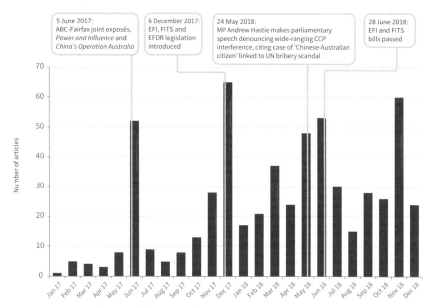

Source: Factiva search string {Chinese influence}.

media's discussions of 'Chinese influence' and the progress of the legislative response.

The package of laws introduced several policy measures that have helped to mitigate risks arising from PRC political activities. In particular, they strengthened prohibitions on covert lobbying on behalf of foreign principals, outlawed various sophisticated techniques deployed by the CCP to suppress dissent and created transparency requirements for former senior officials taking on consultancy work for foreign principals.[35] They also signalled a political intent to tackle problematic CCP activities, and have prompted a series of more focused initiatives in sectors such as universities

---

[34] Hastie, 'What is to be Done?', p. 42; Hartcher, 'Red Flag', p. 67; Diamond and Schell, 'Chinese Influence and American Interests', pp. 148–50.

[35] Techniques intended to be criminalised under the law include: state-directed suppressive counter-protests; threats of harm to family members based overseas; threats to businesses; and threats of visa denial. See 'EFI Law (Aus)', 92.2 and Explanatory Memorandum, pp. 163–66; Australian Government, *Annual Report on the Operation of the Foreign Influence Transparency Scheme* (Canberra: Attorney-General's Department, 2019), pp. 4–5.

and social media.[36] However, critics have argued the drafting of the new laws was rushed and lacked the necessary consultation and review processes.[37] Concerns have persisted over the laws' radical expansion of the legal scope of national security, as well as their effectiveness, particularly in countering interference with diaspora communities' political rights.

Unclear Effectiveness

Although Australian government officials emphasised the urgency of passing the EFI Law to counter 'unprecedented' levels of existing foreign interference, it has so far produced few tangible results. As of March 2021, only one individual had been charged under the law, despite political pressure for counter-interference 'scalps' and more than AUD$87 million in increased funding for counter-interference enforcement announced in December 2019.[38] Huang Xiangmo, one of the PRC businessmen at the centre of the political donations scandal, had his visa revoked on character grounds in January 2019, using pre-existing discretionary powers.[39] Roger Uren, the subject of the Australian Security Intelligence Organisation (ASIO) raid that opened the ABC's *Power and Influence* programme, was charged in October

---

[36] See, for example, Parliament of Australia, 'Select Committee on Foreign Interference Through Social Media', <www.aph.gov.au/Parliamentary_Business/Committees/Senate/Foreign_Interference_through_Social_Media>, accessed 2 April 2021; Australian Government Department of Education, Skills and Employment, 'Establishment of a University Foreign Interference Taskforce', 29 August 2019, <www.education.gov.au/news/establishment-university-foreign-interference-taskforce>, accessed 22 March 2021.

[37] *Hansard (Australian Parliament)*, 'National Security Legislation Amendment (Espionage and Foreign Interference) Bill 2017', Hearing of Parliamentary Joint Committee on Intelligence and Security, Melbourne, 16 March 2018, pp. 10–11; Evelyn Douek, 'What's in Australia's New Laws on Foreign Interference in Domestic Politics?', *Lawfare*, 11 July 2018; Tony Walker, 'Government Needs to Slow Down on Changes to Spying and Foreign Interference Laws', *The Conversation*, 8 June 2018; Paddy Manning, 'Sabotaging Democracy: Espionage and Foreign Interference Laws are Being Rushed Through', *Monthly Today*, 27 June 2018.

[38] Nino Bucci, 'Sunny Duong, Accused of Having Links to Beijing, Vows to Fight Foreign Interference Charge', *The Guardian*, 6 November 2020; Andrew Greene, 'Chinese Spying Allegations Increase Pressure on National Security Community to Claim Scalps', *ABC News*, 26 November 2019. The 2019/20 budget announced $34.8 million over four years, followed by $87.8 million over five years announced in December 2019.

[39] Dan Conifer and Stephanie Boris, 'Australia Denies Citizenship to Chinese Political Donor Huang Xiangmo and Strips His Permanent Residency', *ABC News*, 6 February 2019.

2019 under legislation in place since 2001.[40] A June 2020 counter-interference raid on the homes and offices of New South Wales state backbencher Shaoquett Moselmane and his part-time staffer John Zhang has not resulted in any charges; the investigation remains ongoing as of June 2021.[41]

Hastie has stated that 'protect[ing] diaspora groups from coercion by foreign state actors' was 'precisely why the Coalition government passed foreign interference laws in 2018'.[42] Yet cases of extra-territorial coercion have continued to surface since the laws were passed.[43] While generally supporting the political signal the EFI Law conveyed, multiple members of émigré communities told the author the law had done little to help ease the PRC pressure.[44] Prosecutions for foreign interference against the rights of Chinese dissidents and persecuted minority groups such as Uyghurs and Tibetans appear particularly unlikely due to shortcomings in the design of the legislation. The law's criminalisation of foreign interference against 'Australian democratic political rights' appears only to apply where the targets are Australian citizens, leaving a significant loophole for authoritarian regimes and their supporters to continue coercing overseas students and recent migrants, potentially including political refugees.[45]

The implementation of the Foreign Influence Transparency Scheme also encountered a series of problems. After its launch in December 2018, the scheme prompted registrations from several former officials working for foreign interests, but none from United Front-aligned groups or CIs.[46] Experts criticised the legislation as overly complex, noting that lawyers were offering clients conflicting advice on whether they needed to register, and the Attorney-General's Department struggled to provide clear guidance to the public.[47] In 2019,

---

[40] Elizabeth Byrne and Matthew Doran, 'Former Intelligence Official Roger Uren Facing 30 Charges for Breaching National Secrecy', *ABC News*, 24 October 2019.

[41] Jamelle Wells, 'Shaoquett Moselmane Staffer John Zhang Lodges High Court Challenge to Investigation into Chinese Interference', *ABC News*, 5 August 2020.

[42] Fergus Hunter, 'A Student Attended a Protest at an Australian Uni. Days Later Chinese Officials Visited His Family', *Sydney Morning Herald*, 7 August 2019.

[43] Dirk Van Der Kley, 'What Should Australia Do About … The Influence of United Front Work?', *China Matters Explores*, September 2020.

[44] Author interviews with five émigré community members based in Australia, April–May 2020. The platforms through which these communications took place have been withheld to protect the sources.

[45] The term 'Australian democratic political right' is intended to refer 'only to rights that arise because of a person's status as Australian'. See 'EFI Law (Aus)', Explanatory Memorandum, pp. 92, 163, 169.

[46] Anthony Galloway, 'Foreign Interference Scheme Targets Just One Potential Agent of Influence', *Sydney Morning Herald*, 28 November 2019.

Attorney-General Christian Porter criticised his own department when it asked former Prime Minister Tony Abbott to register under the scheme after he spoke at a think tank event co-organised with a US conservative group.[48] A new unit was created to administer the scheme in March 2020.[49]

Campaign finance experts have identified serious shortcomings in the EFDR Law.[50] The law did not prohibit donations from Australia-based subsidiaries of foreign companies, nor cap donations at a level that would prevent undue influence from being generated.[51] Critics have noted that the EFDR Law did not even preclude continued donations by either of the two CCP-linked businessmen at the centre of the media exposés and security agencies' concerns.[52] Nor did it address the lack of disclosure obligations for donations of up to AUD$14,000, the long lag time for reporting of donations above that amount and a number of other related issues.[53] These examples suggest how seeking to address various complex issues in a single legislative surge amid heated public rhetoric and media coverage can impact on the new laws' fitness for purpose.

---

[47] Fact sheets explaining the scheme to the public were released in draft form and later required correction. Author enquiry to Attorney-General's Department (AGD), 8 December 2018. Former Prime Minister Kevin Rudd has complained publicly of receiving indeterminate advice from the AGD on the question of which of his own activities he needed to register: 'The Morrison Government's definition of a foreign "arrangement" is so broad, they reckon I may be at risk of becoming a secret agent of British influence in Australia just by appearing live on @BBC. Even if Australia doesn't come up. Or even if I criticise the UK Govt on-air', <https://twitter.com/MrKRudd/status/1341870469880795137>, accessed 22 March 2021.

[48] Max Koslowski, 'Foreign Influence Laws Won't Change After Tony Abbott Targeted, Porter Says', *Sydney Morning Herald*, 5 November 2019.

[49] Anthony Galloway, 'Suspected Foreign Agents Ordered to Hand Over Documents as New Unit Targets China Links', *Sydney Morning Herald*, 7 March 2020.

[50] Yee-fui Ng, 'The Foreign Donations Bill Will Soon Be Law – What Will it Do, and Why Is it Needed?' *The Conversation*, 28 November 2018.

[51] Paul Karp, 'Coalition Bill to Ban Foreign Political Donations Passes Senate', *The Guardian*, 15 November 2018.

[52] Ng, 'The Foreign Donations Bill Will Soon Be Law – What Will it Do, and Why is it Needed?'.

[53] Centre for Public Integrity, 'Hidden Money in Politics: What the AEC Disclosures Don't Tell Us', Briefing Paper, February 2020, <publicintegrity.org.au/wp-content/uploads/2020/02/Briefing-paper-Hidden-money-in-politics-2019.pdf>; Danielle Wood and Kate Griffiths, 'Who's in the Room? Access and Influence in Australian Politics', Grattan Institute Report No. 12, 2018, p. 45.

Diminishment of Civil Liberties

The Turnbull government's legislative package attracted hundreds of written objections from Australian and international civil society. The UN Special Rapporteurs on human rights and democratic freedoms were 'gravely concerned that the Bill would impose draconian criminal penalties on expression and access to information that is central to public debate and accountability in a democratic society'. Human Rights Watch flagged the EFI bill's potential to 'encroach upon freedom of political communication and a free press'. Greenpeace argued the new laws would 'have the effect of criminalising public participation in Australia's democracy'.[54]

Legal experts were particularly concerned with the finalised EFI Law's expansion of the scope of 'national security' to include Australia's 'political, military or economic relations with another country'. The Law Council of Australia pointed out that such broad definitions undermine the rule of law, which depends on clarity of rules, especially in relation to serious crimes.[55] The effect was to bring a large but undefined array of new matters within the scope of national security.[56] In particular, Human Rights Watch and Amnesty International argued that it risked criminalising the revelation of human rights violations or illegal conduct by Australian government agencies.[57]

While Canberra presented foreign interference as the key rationale for the EFI Law, a large majority of its content was concerned with other matters, including espionage, treason and government secrecy. In total only around 10% of the law's content was devoted to foreign interference

---

[54] See the full lists of submissions: <www.aph.gov.au/Parliamentary_Business/Committees/Joint/Intelligence_and_Security/TransparencySchemeBill/Submissions>, accessed 22 March 2021; <www.aph.gov.au/Parliamentary_Business/Committees/Joint/Intelligence_and_Security/EspionageFInterference/Submissions>, accessed 22 March 2021.

[55] *Hansard (Australian Parliament)*, 'National Security Legislation Amendment (Espionage and Foreign Interference), Bill 2017', pp. 10–11; author telephone interview with Attorney-General's Department staff, 7 February 2019.

[56] EFI Law, 90.4(1)e; Human Rights Law Centre, 'Response to Amendments Proposed by the Attorney-General's Department', 14 March 2018, p. 7, <static1.squarespace.com/static/580025f66b8f5b2dabbe4291/t/5aa86b72e2c4839970023836/1520986999078/Human+Rights+Law+Centre+-+Supplementary+Submission+to+the+Inquiry+into+the+National+Security+Legislation+Amendment+%28EFI%29+Bill+2017+-+14+March+2018.pdf>, accessed 22 March 2021.

[57] Elaine Pearson, 'Australia's Government Must Guard Against Foreign Interference, But Not by Curbing Our Rights', *ABC News*, 14 June 2018; Paul Karp, 'Espionage Bill Could Make Some Protests Criminal Acts, Getup Says', *The Guardian*, 26 June 2018.

(pp. 19–20 and 36–42), compared with around 40% in the sections on espionage, treason and other similar offences (pp. 4–54) and 25% on secrecy (pp. 54–79). Transparency advocates contended the secrecy provisions were aimed at would-be whistleblowers, while civil society groups argued new sabotage offences criminalised peaceful protest.[58] The law also raised new risks to researchers and civil society advocates interacting professionally with government officials by introducing a new crime of 'dealing with' classified information, carrying up to two years in prison.[59] Journalists in Australia – who, as noted above, were credited with creating the conditions for the law's introduction and eventual passing – would have been subject to the same penalty, but for an amendment allowing a legal defence for media personnel.[60]

The Law Council of Australia also criticised the drafting of the FITS Law, arguing it contained vague language that could generate a chilling effect on participation in public affairs.[61] Australians advancing independently formed views on public affairs could be required to register under the scheme if they have previously interacted with a 'foreign principal' over the issue at hand; no influence on the content of those views is necessary, nor any material support or instruction.[62]

---

[58]   Greenpeace Australia Pacific, 'Submission to the Review of the Espionage and Foreign Interference Bill 2017', 15 March 2018, p. 2; Karp, 'Espionage Bill Could Make Some Protests Criminal Acts, Getup Says'; Human Rights Law Centre, 'Parliament Votes to Introduce New Secrecy and Espionage Offences', 7 June 2018.

[59]   EFI Law, 122.4A. Hearing classified information, whether fact or opinion, could constitute a crime with a two-year jail term. The law does not require that such information is shared – or is intended to be shared – with any foreign country, nor does it allow any defence for professional conduct in good faith and in the public interest, as recommended by the Law Council of Australia. Lawyers from the Attorney-General's Department argued public interest defence is unnecessary because 'it can never be in the public interest' for outsiders to deal with information they know, or should know, is classified. Author email communication with Attorney-General Department lawyers, 5 February 2019.

[60]   The amendment allowing a defence for 'media personnel' has been criticised by legal experts as insufficiently specific. See Law Council of Australia, 'Espionage Report a Step in the Right Direction', 8 June 2018.

[61]   The Law Council of Australia argued that vague language in the legislation would risk a 'chilling of otherwise legitimate and constructive advocacy'. See Law Council of Australia, 'Foreign Influence Transparency Scheme Bill 2017', 22 January 2018, p. 8; Douek, 'What's in Australia's New Laws on Foreign Interference in Domestic Politics?'; Australian Lawyers for Human Rights, 'Position Statement: Foreign Influence Transparency Scheme', March 2018, pp. 12–13.

[62]   The Attorney-General's Department offered the hypothetical example of an Australian blogger writing about a policy issue who is then contacted by a foreign principal encouraging her to continue. Any subsequent writing on the issue could be considered to be issued 'under an arrangement with' the foreign principal because the two parties shared an awareness that such activity would occur. See

Ordinary individuals from countries ruled by repressive regimes could meet the definition of a 'foreign principal', potentially creating registration obligations for Australians who interact with them.[63] Refusing to register is a criminal offence carrying up to five years' jail time.[64]

These wide-ranging concerns from Australian civil society regarding the Turnbull government's legislative responses reflect the challenge of protecting national security and political rights in a liberal democracy in an era of growing PRC power. Media coverage raising public concern about pervasive 'Chinese influence' generated both an urgent political impetus for action and a compressed timeframe for drafting and enacting new laws – circumstances unconducive to the methodical weighing of competing values and crafting of policies that minimise or avoid collateral damage.[65] Australia's new laws have been held up in North

---

Attorney-General's Department, 'Foreign Influence Transparency Scheme: Factsheet 16 (Draft)', December 2018. This was subsequently confirmed in author email and telephone communications with the Attorney-General's Department, 18 December 2018 and 28 January 2019. In an updated version of the Factsheet scenario, published in February 2019, the foreign government grants the blogger an exclusive interview with one of its political figures. Subsequent blogging on the topic will be registrable: 'Although [hypothetical Australian writer] Jane is writing her own thoughts on the policy, there is an arrangement with a foreign government to undertake a communications activity intended to influence an Australian Government process (i.e. the acceptance of the offer of an interview and agreement to continue blogging on the issue). As such, she must register under the scheme and ensure that both her blog posts and Tweets include the required disclosure'. See Attorney-General's Department, 'Foreign Influence Transparency Scheme: Factsheet 11', February 2019.

[63] Under the FITS Law, Section 10, 'foreign principal' is not limited to governments or state-run entities, but also covers individuals who are 'accustomed, or under an obligation (whether formal or informal)' to act in accordance with the 'wishes' of a foreign government. Paragraph 100 of the FITS Supplementary Explanatory Memorandum specifies that the definition 'will not apply to obligations with which all persons are obliged or accustomed to comply. For example, all persons are under an obligation to obey the law of a foreign country, and this will not be sufficient'. Advice from an AGD legal team adds that 'there would need to be additional facts and circumstances applying specifically to an individual and their relationship with a foreign government, political party or government related entity'. Author email communication with AGD legal team, 21 March 2019. Given the formal control over social science research by China and other authoritarian regimes such as Vietnam, Australian-based researchers who publish articles after holding meetings with counterparts from such countries could be undertaking registrable communications activities.

[64] FITS Law, Section 57.

[65] One interviewee from the Australian legal profession stated, 'Normally, you would expect an overarching review for such serious offences, normally it would get at least referred to the ALRC [Australian Law Reform Commission], to hear from both prosecuting and defending agencies, and others who may be affected

America and Europe as an exemplary response to the PRC's overseas political activities, but it is not clear that the benefits of their rapid enactment have outweighed what the country's peak legal body described as a 'leap into the unknown for freedom of speech'.[66]

Misaligned Institutional Responsibilities

Australia's national security community has taken a leading role in both public discourse on PRC interference and the development of policy countermeasures. There are two identifiable downsides, however, both of which relate closely to the issues of inflammatory public discourse and overreaching legislation discussed above. One is that national security agencies may be less than ideally suited to handling issues such as encroachments on civil liberties. Rolling the protection of the rights of individuals and minority groups into an aggregated national security task set that also includes countering threats to the integrity of government risks positioning the most impactful PRC overseas political activities as secondary concerns. Another is the role of intelligence agencies in the public policy discourse. In Australia, the prominence of anonymously-sourced national security information in setting the public agenda has made it difficult to achieve transparency and facilitate public scrutiny of the evidence base upon which major policy decisions are to be made.

Functional Mismatches

While some proponents of the EFI Law in Canberra have drawn much-needed attention to the stories of Chinese dissidents facing PRC harassment and coercion overseas, the law's sections on interference with political rights were only a minor part of its content. As noted above, the majority of the law dealt instead with espionage, treason and secrecy. In fact, a criminal offence of 'interference with political liberties' had already existed in Australia since 1914.[67] Since its passage through parliament, the Australian government has established a cross-departmental National Counter Foreign Interference Taskforce, under the National Counter Foreign Interference Coordinator (NCFIC), who is an officer from the Australian Security Intelligence Organisation (ASIO) seconded to the Department of Home Affairs. This arrangement makes

---

by it. This, however, was referred to Home Affairs, which has a vested interest in all of this, which prepared the legislation, released in December, with replies [required] by January'. Author telephone interview with Australian legal expert, February 2019.

[66] Law Council of Australia, 'Espionage Report a Step in the Right Direction'.

[67] EFI Law, pp. 19–20.

sense for national security tasks such as countering threats of electoral interference and covert cultivation of politicians by foreign agents, but is not an adequate means of upholding civil rights of members of diaspora communities. The NCFIC has so far had little public profile, and the primary focus of the role appears to have been on sovereignty and security.[68]

The subordinate position of political rights of migrant communities within the Australian government's concept of foreign interference was evident in its 2017 Foreign Policy White Paper, which discussed foreign interference only in relation to 'sovereign institutions and decision-making', and did not mention democratic rights of diaspora community members.[69] The Counter Foreign Interference Strategy (CFIS), announced in 2019, indicated little change in this regard, referring to interference with 'political and government institutions' and 'private sector decision making' but not political rights.[70] The CFIS does list 'engag[ing] at-risk sectors to raise awareness and develop mitigation strategies' as one of its 'five pillars' of counter-interference, though the extent to which this involves engagement with diaspora communities is not clear.[71] The NCFIC's 'Countering Foreign Interference' website states that 'enhancing engagement with culturally and linguistically diverse communities to strengthen their ability to challenge manipulation and coercion from foreign actors' is one of its tasks.[72] Yet it provides no information for

---

[68] See *Hansard (Australian Parliament)*, 22 October 2018, p. 199. The NCFIC follows the government's Counter Foreign Interference (CFI) Strategy, with the stated aim of '[p]rotecting Australia's sovereignty, values and national interests'. The goal of protecting the free speech rights of members of diaspora communities is presumably contained within the 'values' element. See Australian Government, Department of Home Affairs, 'National Counter Foreign Interference Coordinator', 19 August 2019, <www.homeaffairs.gov.au/about-us/our-portfolios/national-security/countering-foreign-interference/cfi-coordinator>, accessed 22 March 2021; civil society organisations specialising in human rights were not consulted on the role of NCFIC. Author telephone interview with civil society organisation executive, 24 January 2019.

[69] Australian Government, *2017 Foreign Policy White Paper*, pp. 75–76.

[70] Australian Government, Department of Home Affairs, 'Australia's Counter Foreign Interference Strategy'.

[71] According to one community leader, nearly two years after the passing of the laws no significant outreach efforts had been made to the Australian Uyghur community regarding foreign interference. Author interview, May 2020 (platform withheld).

[72] Australian Government, Department of Home Affairs, 'National Counter Foreign Interference Coordinator'.

members of such communities wishing to initiate such engagement, nor any resources in languages other than English.

As of March 2021, the Countering Foreign Interference website features no advice or contacts for individuals who have been subject to foreign interference against their political rights in Australia. The site's contact section only appeals for tipoffs to the National Security Hotline, and suggests crimes be reported to local police and Crime Stoppers.[73] The 'resources' section is limited to links to five pieces of complex and specialised English-language legislation. One of the counter-interference strategy's early public-facing products, 'Guidelines to Counter Foreign Interference in the Australian University Sector', released in November 2019, addressed issues such as due diligence in research collaborations, intellectual property, development of dual-use technologies and cyber security, but did not mention interference with political rights (or academic freedom) on university campuses.[74] These observations indicate that countering foreign interference against civil liberties is a relatively low priority compared with the national security aspects of foreign interference. A disaggregated approach locating rights protection tasks outside the national security establishment would likely be more effective in addressing interference against democratic rights by the PRC and other foreign states.

Opaque Information Releases

In 2016, the Turnbull government commissioned a classified report on PRC interference in Australian politics, to be jointly prepared by the Prime Minister's Office and ASIO.[75] The document reportedly formed a significant element of the evidence base for the legislation discussed above, but only fragments were made public via apparently authorised leaks to the media. In the words of one former Australian official, rather than shining sunlight on the important issues surrounding the PRC's political activities in Australia, Canberra's information releases provided only 'intermittent flickers of a 30-watt globe'.[76]

---

[73] Interviewees from Australian PRC dissident and minority communities noted that the counter-interference initiatives had not made it easier for those suffering CCP harassment to get help. Author interviews with émigré community members, April and May 2020.

[74] Australian Government, University Foreign Interference Taskforce, 'Guidelines to Counter Foreign Interference in the Australian University Sector', November 2019.

[75] Chris Uhlmann, 'Top-Secret Report Uncovers High-Level Chinese Interference in Australian Politics', 9 News, 28 May 2018.

[76] Author telephone interview with former Australian public servant, June 2018.

The major media splashes that drove the 'Chinese influence' discourse to national prominence explicitly channelled the views of anonymous security personnel. The ABC's *Power and Influence* investigation attributed its narrative of an urgent threat to Australian sovereignty to beliefs of 'the defence and intelligence community'.[77] *Power and Influence* was only the most prominent of a series of media reports conveying a sense of frustration expressed by Australian security officials in anonymous briefings from 2016 until the passage of the new laws in mid-2018.[78] In many cases reports based on claims by anonymous officials produced alarmist headlines depicting pervasive espionage and subversion carried out by everyday Chinese people, described in one headline as 'citizen spies'.[79]

There is little doubt that the Australian media reports regarding the sentiments of senior national security officials were accurate. Duncan Lewis, Australia's director-general of security from 2015 to 2019, expressed a sense of cooperation with the media over the issue:

> There has been a great deal of coverage recently in the Australian media regarding espionage and foreign interference, ascribing blame and describing vectors of attack and influence. It's not proper for me to dive into the detail of the individual cases and the coverage of these events for very obvious reasons. Suffice it to say I am satisfied that ASIO is following the ball very closely. We have seeded what is now a public consciousness, and an awareness of the matter, and I hope in short order there will come an increased public preparedness to defend our country and its sovereignty.[80]

In an interview published shortly after his retirement, Lewis declared foreign interference, overwhelmingly from China, to be an 'existential threat' to Australia that 'takes over, basically, pulling the strings from offshore'.[81]

The necessarily secretive nature of defence and security agencies' work makes it difficult for them to engage in public policy debates openly. Anonymous injections of national security information into the public discourse poses risks to the public policymaking process, to the

---

[77] Nick McKenzie et al., 'Australian Sovereignty Under Threat from Influence of China's Communist Party', *ABC News*, 6 June 2017.

[78] See Chris Uhlmann, 'Australian Businesses with Close Ties to China Donated $5.5m to Political Parties, Investigation Shows', *ABC News*, 22 August 2016.

[79] Aaron Patrick, 'Australia is Losing the Battle Against China's "Citizen Spies"', *Australian Financial Review*, 3 September 2016.

[80] Lewis, 'Address to the Lowy Institute'.

[81] Hartcher, 'Red Flag', pp. 25, 36.

quality of public debates and to citizens' rights to reliable political information. Such sources cannot be held accountable for their claims, and the evidence with which to evaluate their veracity is absent, as when former FBI Director J Edgar Hoover leaked security information to the press, degrading US public debates over national security during the Cold War.[82] Even where collective conclusions of the Australian intelligence community have been stated officially, such as the 'unprecedented scale' of foreign espionage and interference, no evidence has been provided for the claim.[83]

As noted above, proponents of Australia's expanded national security laws consider the media discourse to have paved the way for the legislative response discussed above. The laws' most controversial elements, in turn, reflected Australian security agencies' preferences. ASIO advocated in favour of the expansive, elastic definition of national security established by the EFI Law, on the grounds that the concept has an 'elusive definition' and 'depends on what is actually a threat to the nation at any given time'.[84] ASIO also opposed defences in the legislation for journalists, researchers and activists, including those acting in good faith in the public interest, on the grounds that many professions make good cover for foreign spies.[85] Apart from the inclusion of a defence for media personnel reporting in the public interest, the finalised laws followed these recommendations.

Conclusion

Australia's public policy discourse over the PRC's political activities, the expansive national security legislation passed in response, and the non-transparent role of intelligence agencies in the process, were closely interrelated developments, as Figure 4 illustrates. The effect of their interaction has been to raise significant risks to Australia's civil liberties, social cohesion and even national security itself. Hastie has argued that, through its media discourse and legislative response, Australia is 'a helpful case study of a democracy that has taken action to protect itself'

---

[82] See Caute, *The Great Fear*, pp. 113–14.

[83] Bevan Shields, 'ASIO Chief Duncan Lewis Sounds Fresh Alarm Over Foreign Interference Threat', *Sydney Morning Herald*, 24 May 2018.

[84] *Hansard (Australian Parliament)*, 'National Security Legislation Amendment (Espionage and Foreign Interference) Bill 2017', p. 44.

[85] *Ibid.*, pp. 35–37. Making clear that China was the principal concern, Lewis offered examples of the threat from 'a foreign power using local Australians to observe and harass its diaspora community' and 'recruitment and co-opting of influential and powerful Australian voices' for lobbying. See Lewis, 'Address to the Lowy Institute'.

Figure 4: Interlinking of Aggregation-Related Risks

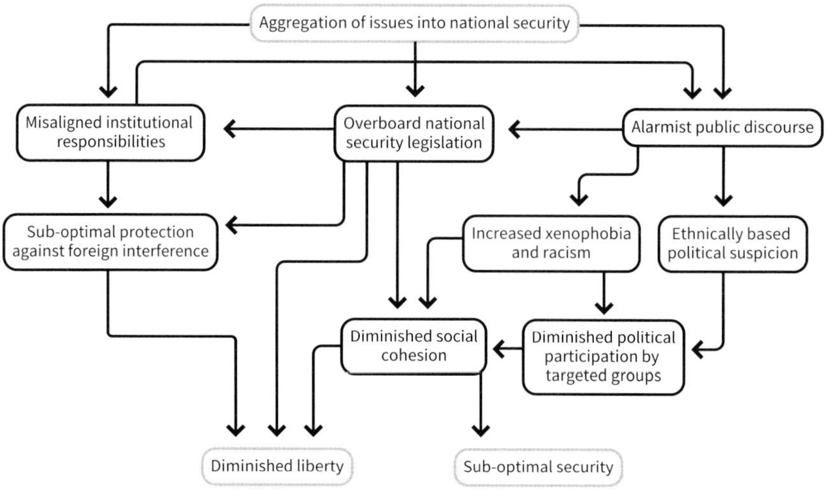

Source: Author generated.

against threats from the PRC.[86] This chapter has indicated that other states would benefit from looking to Australia's response for cautionary as well as salutary lessons. The following chapter turns to how the risks of both inaction and reaction can be managed.

---

[86] Hastie, 'What is to be Done?', p. 41.

IV. MANAGING THE RISKS

With Sino–American geopolitical rivalry escalating, PRC overseas political activities are presenting US-aligned liberal democracies with an array of complex, unavoidable policy issues. Alongside thorny technical questions of economic dependence, defence technology exports and PRC investment in strategic infrastructure, liberal democracies need to wrestle with how to properly manage the array of distinct political challenges presented by the CCP and its supporters' overseas activities. Chapter I showed how faulty terminology has made the challenges difficult to define. Chapter II disaggregated their varying nature, causes, actors and relationship to liberal-democratic principles. Chapter III showed how the need to respond itself generates a further series of risks to social cohesion, civil liberties and national security.

This chapter offers a set of policy suggestions based on a risk-management framework that takes the preservation and strengthening of three core liberal-democratic institutions – integrity of the political system, protection of civil rights of individuals and groups, and academic freedom in research and education – as the immediate and overriding goal of policy measures. As discussed in the Introduction, this contrasts with aggregative approaches that apply a singular national security lens to a wide array of problems, and often take suppressing PRC political activity, or the conduct of 'political warfare', as overriding goals. The disaggregation-based risk-management approach advocated here implies neither permissiveness towards PRC interference, nor neutrality in the incipient systemic competition between democracy and authoritarianism. It reflects instead an underlying assumption that the prospects for liberal democracy in the current global context depend on the strength of liberal-democratic institutions and consistency between liberal-democratic principles and governments' policies and practices.

Common organisational risk-management practice involves a hierarchy of hazard control measures. If it is possible to eliminate a risk entirely, this is the preferred course of action. The next-best alternative is substitution, meaning replacement of the source with a less risky alternative. The third choice is control measures to maximise distance

Figure 5: Risk Management Hierarchy

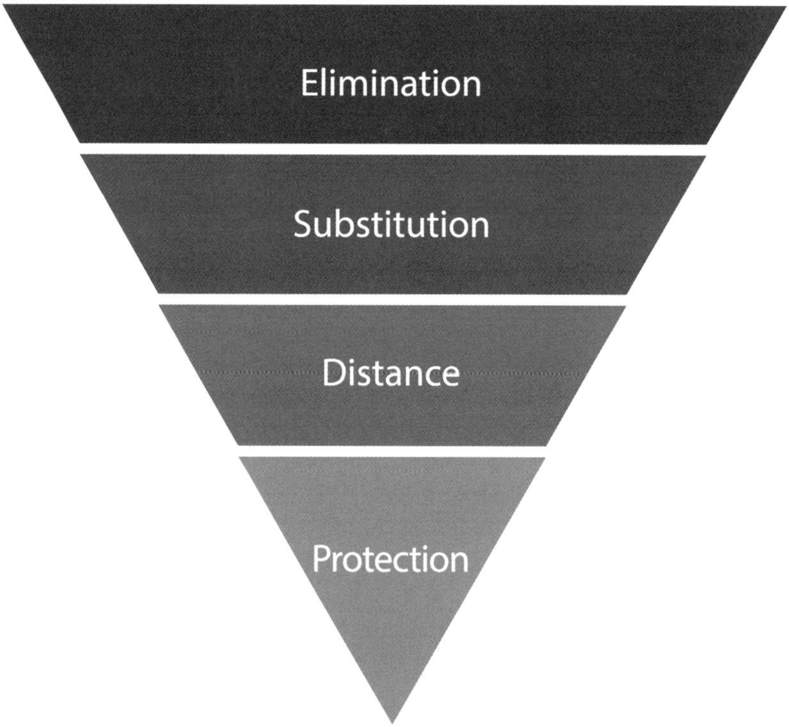

Source: Author generated.

between source of risk and those who would be harmed. Fourth, where exposure to the risk is unavoidable, protections should be employed to mitigate harm.[1] Applying these principles, three sets of measures are suggested below to manage risks to national security, civil liberties and academic freedom. This is not to suggest that these measures are sufficient, nor that each is necessary in every context. Different countries have different combinations of existing measures in place, and priorities for response need to be based on local circumstances. These three sets of suggestions are intended to be illustrative and generative, rather than comprehensive and prescriptive.

A relatively recent development in risk-management theory flows from a broadening of the concept of risk to encompass both the

---

[1] Centers for Disease Control and Prevention, 'Hierarchy of Controls', 13 January 2015.

downside and upside consequences of uncertainty.[2] This usefully places the focus not only on forestalling negative outcomes, but also on seeking to benefit from opportunities that arise from the same risk factors. As we have seen, many of the risks raised by PRC overseas political activities are rooted in broader domestic shortcomings and vulnerabilities. This means the challenges of responding are in many cases also opportunities to fundamentally strengthen liberal-democratic institutions.

National Security Measures

National security issues by nature sit in a special category away from normal politics in a liberal democracy, mandating their handling through investigation and punishments administered to varying degrees in secret. Yet covert and coercive tools are of course not the only necessary means of managing national security risks. Legal and regulative frameworks can adjust individual incentives so as to decrease the likelihood or prevalence of actions that undermine the system's integrity. Public information can facilitate perceptions of integrity upon which the system depends, and targeted elite education can help ensure key individuals understand the often complex and subtle risks that their institutions face.

Enhance China Literacy

Liberal democracies need to institute and maintain rolling programmes of executive education aimed at boosting the overall level of 'China literacy' among politicians, public servants, business and educational leaders. Cultivating elite China literacy requires raising awareness of both the CCP's institutions and strategies, and also of Mainland China's place within the broader Chinese world that includes Hong Kong, Taiwan and local Chinese diaspora communities.[3] Besides reducing the risk of the PRC party-state mediating foreign politicians' relationships with constituents who are members of the Chinese diaspora, this would also generate opportunities to improve the quality and breadth of politicians' community engagement.

---

[2] See International Organization for Standardization (ISO), 'ISO 31000:2009 Risk Management — Principles and Guidelines', November 2009, <https://www.iso.org/standard/43170.html>, accessed 2 April 2021.

[3] Combining education on the PRC with education on China in the world reflects the concept of New Sinology, which advocates approaching the PRC as one aspect of a global 'Sinophone world'. See Geremie Barmé, 'What is New Sinology?', *China Heritage*, <http://chinaheritage.net/reader/what-is-new-sinology>, accessed 22 March 2021.

Many of these issues are matters of ongoing research, so China literacy programmes should not be set up as 'training' exercises designed to simply transfer knowledge. They should aim instead to elevate awareness of, and where appropriate critical engagement with, ongoing controversies and debates in relevant fields of research (such as comparative Marxism-Leninism, politics in Greater China, PRC foreign policy, Chinese history and global diasporas). A critical approach to China literacy programmes would offer a twofold benefit to national security. Most directly, it would help mitigate the risks of elite co-optation by elevating key individuals' ability to make informed judgements regarding their engagements with the PRC in the context of the other 'Chinas' that exist globally. At the same time, it also stands to bolster national security by increasing contestability in intelligence analysis and policymaking processes.

Experts have consistently urged public investment in linguistic and cultural programmes to grow China literacy at the elite and popular level.[4] The PRC's newfound political, military and economic heft have revealed this imperative to be a matter of urgency.[5] Government support for Chinese language, history and culture in schools and universities, as well as human engagement initiatives such as student exchanges, may become politically difficult as geopolitical tensions stifle engagement across various sectors, especially business and high-tech research. However, such pressure also presents opportunities to enrich what have often been narrow, instrumentalist notions of China engagement – such as viewing government-to-government China engagement solely through the lens of relations with the PRC party-state, and 'people-to-people' links as constituted by tourism and education exports. In a world of incipient geopolitical rivalry, humanistic engagement in areas such as language, arts and literature, politics and philosophy are increasingly important, as are scientific and policy collaboration on global challenges like climate change.

Caps on Political Donations
The risk of a corrupting influence from foreign political donations is part of a broader problem of money in liberal-democratic politics. The UK currently has no limit on permissible domestic political donations, and

---

[4] See Stephen FitzGerald, *Is Australia an Asian Country? Can Australia Survive in an East Asian Future?* (Sydney: Allen & Unwin, 1997); Geremie Barmé, 'Australia and China in the World: Whose Literacy?', *China Heritage Quarterly* (No. 27, 2011).
[5] Bates Gill and Linda Jakobson, *China Matters: Getting it Right for Australia* (Carlton: Black Inc., 2017), p. 192; Jaivin, 'The New Era'.

allows anonymous donations of up to £7,500.[6] A general cap on political donations, coupled with public funding of political parties, would be the simplest way to eliminate the risk of corrupting donations while also improving public confidence in the integrity of the system.[7] In the absence of such reforms, prohibiting or capping foreign-source donations is essential to protect democratic political systems from undue foreign influence-buying and elite co-optation and, equally importantly, the perception thereof. Australia's EFDR Law has capped foreign political donations at AUD$100, while the UK currently allows foreign donations of up to £500. However, as noted in Chapter III, Australia's legislation does not stop foreign companies' wholly-owned subsidiaries from donating. The UK's rules, meanwhile, allow subsidiaries of foreign companies to donate as domestic donors, provided the money is generated in the UK.[8] None of these rules apply, of course, to local citizens and residents who may share overlapping interests or maintain close relationships with foreign governments. Thus, while caps on foreign donations may be necessary, only a more general cap on political donations can effectively eliminate this channel of potential foreign influence.

Public Information on Electoral Integrity
Despite intense speculation about possible PRC interference in Australian by-elections between 2017 and 2018, and a general election in 2019, including from government ministers, no authoritative information has been forthcoming on whether this occurred, and if so, in what form. Without authoritative, non-partisan information, such speculation risks feeding public perceptions of the system as compromised at a time when faith in democratic processes has been shaken among citizens, following Russian interference in US and UK votes.[9] Governments should provide clear, non-partisan and timely information on the actual situation of the

---

[6] The Electoral Commission, 'Overview of Donations to Political Parties', p. 6, <https://www.electoralcommission.org.uk/i-am-a/party-or-campaigner/political-parties/guidance-reporting-donations-and-loans-great-britain>, accessed 22 March 2021; Joe Langstaffe, 'Political Parties Anonymous Donation "Loophole" Criticised", *BBC News*, 21 March 2021.

[7] Joo-cheong Tham, 'Better Regulation of All Political Finance Would Help Control Foreign Donations', *The Conversation*, 1 September 2016; Ng, 'The Foreign Donations Bill Will Soon Be Law – What Will it Do, and Why Is it Needed?'.

[8] Claire Feikert-Ahalt, 'Regulation of Foreign Involvement in Elections: Great Britain', Library of Congress, August 2019.

[9] Intelligence and Security Committee, *Russia*, pp. 9–10.

country's electoral integrity to protect and strengthen public confidence. The Australian government has set up an Electoral Integrity Assurance Taskforce, bringing together national security agencies and the Australian Electoral Commission, but its website has so far contained only sporadic information on specific threats to electoral integrity.[10] The UK announced a 'Defending Democracy' programme in mid-2019 aimed at boosting public confidence in democratic institutions, but in the words of the Intelligence and Security Committee it 'seems to have been afforded a rather low priority'.[11] The programme also lacks a public-facing presence. Regular reports of the relative level and type of observed foreign interference attempts across electoral cycles would help citizens identify and contextualise the various threats that exist, and boost confidence in the integrity of the system.

Timely Donation Disclosures

The rise of United Front-affiliated and other pro-PRC donors has highlighted a more general need for timely disclosure of donations, gifts and other benefits to political actors. Australia's FITS Law helpfully introduced stringent disclosure requirements on former ministers and senior public servants working on behalf of foreign interests. The UK currently prohibits ex-ministers from all lobbying activity for two years after leaving office, a period that government could consider extending.[12] But timely public information on donations to political parties as well as gifts and in-kind benefits to individual politicians is still notably lacking in Australia as disclosures are released annually. In the UK, political donations are reported monthly.[13] A publicly accessible real-time register of donations to political parties and benefits conferred on former senior ministers and public servants would help to provide protections to the integrity of the system by enabling the media and general public to monitor political party funding and lobbying activities more closely.[14] In

---

[10] Australian Electoral Taskforce, 'Electoral Integrity Assurance Taskforce', <www.aec.gov.au/elections/electoral-advertising/electoral-integrity.htm>, accessed 22 March 2021.
[11] Intelligence and Security Committee, *Russia*, p. 12.
[12] Cabinet Office, 'Ministerial Code', 23 August 2019, <https://www.gov.uk/government/publications/ministerial-code>, accessed 22 March 2021.
[13] The Electoral Commission, 'Latest UK Political Party Donations and Loans Published', 3 December 2020, <https://www.electoralcommission.org.uk/media-centre/latest-uk-political-party-donations-and-loans-published-0>, accessed 22 March 2021.
[14] Wood and Griffiths, 'Who's in the Room?'; Centre for Public Integrity, 'Eliminating the Undue Influence of Money in Politics', Discussion Paper, September 2019.

addition, more frequent and easily accessible reporting requirements for gifts and other interests could help reduce the incidence of elite co-optation via material benefits.[15]

Clear Definitions in National Security Legislation

The rule of law requires that legislative responses to PRC overseas political activities are based on precise terminology. The expansive definition of 'national security' in Australia's EFI Law, combined with the lack of public interest defences for whistleblowers, civil society organisations and researchers, has raised the risk that governments could seek to deter the exposure of serious wrongdoing and pursue serious charges against critics – outcomes that would challenge the integrity of liberal-democratic systems.[16] To control the possibility of future misuse of national security legislation, liberal-democratic governments should ensure the terms of national security legislation are tightly and clearly defined, and provide defences for dealing with information in the public interest.[17]

Greater Accountability in National Security Reporting

Information from anonymous government sources has been central to Australia's 'Chinese influence' discussion. This has often made it difficult for citizens to evaluate the veracity of the information and the government's own role in the public discourse. Existing media ethics codes typically require that anonymous sources be avoided if possible, and close consideration given to their possible motives.[18] These should be updated to reflect the challenges presented by the proliferation in the use

---

[15] Centre for Public Integrity, 'Eliminating the Undue Influence of Money in Politics', pp. 4–5.

[16] See Human Rights Watch, 'Submission 30', PJCIS Inquiry into the Impact of the Exercise of Law Enforcement and Intelligence Powers on the Freedom of the Press, 2 August 2019; the prosecution of lawyer Bernard Collaery, who represented the former ASIS whistleblower who exposed an operation to eavesdrop on Timor-Leste's cabinet room for commercial advantage, is suggestive of the risk. See Steve Cannane, 'Secrets, Spies and Trials', *Four Corners*, *ABC News*, 26 August 2019, <https://www.aph.gov.au/Parliamentary_Business/Committees/Joint/Intelligence_and_Security/EspionageFInterference/Submissions>, accessed 22 March 2021.

[17] See Human Rights Watch, 'Submission 30'; Commonwealth of Australia, Australian Law Reform Commission, *Secrecy Laws and Open Government in Australia*, Report No. 112 (Canberra: Attorney-General's Department, 2009).

[18] Society of Professional Journalists, 'Anonymous Sources', SPJ Ethics Committee Position Papers, <www.spj.org/ethics-papers-anonymity.asp>, accessed 22 March 2021; Media, Entertainment and Arts Alliance, 'MEAA Journalist Code of Ethics', <www.meaa.org/meaa-media/code-of-ethics>, accessed 22 March 2021.

of such anonymous sources in recent years. Reports carrying anonymous government information should explain to readers why the source has been granted anonymity. While journalists cannot reveal their confidential sources, they should be transparent to readers about the decisions they make in granting anonymity. Online reporting platforms, in particular, can introduce footnotes justifying each decision to carry anonymous information.

Civil Liberties

Mitigating, controlling and where possible eliminating the complex risks to the political rights of diaspora communities and the public at large requires a set of measures matched to the specifics of each issue. Laws can and should ensure appropriate penalties and diplomatic sanctions are applied to foreign state personnel and agents who coerce others on the basis of political views. But countering such encroachments also requires accessible channels through which members of targeted communities can both report such issues and receive advice on mitigation. Meanwhile, modest funding allocations and new disclosure requirements could help to offset distortions that have emerged in the Chinese-language information environment.

Penalties for Extra-Territorial Political Coercion

Democratic governments should seek to ensure that the full range of modern techniques of coercion are prohibited under the law, and that penalties apply to individual officials who order or implement such coercion from abroad. As noted in Chapter III, techniques addressed in Australia's 2018 EFI Law included threats to a person's relatives in another country, of financial punishment, of visa denial and suppressive counter-protests. However, the law apparently outlawed such conduct only insofar as it interfered with the rights of Australian nationals, a status that many of the most vulnerable targets, such as recent migrants or refugees, do not have. Liberal democracies should make sure citizens and non-citizens alike have legal protections against these and other techniques of interference against at-risk populations. It is vital, too, that legislative protections are communicated effectively to culturally and linguistically diverse communities via multilingual websites, community outreach and clear contact points (see next section).

Often, authoritarian states' acts of interference with political rights occur offshore (such as against the families of overseas dissidents or minority groups), and thus outside the sovereign jurisdiction of liberal democracies. A register of foreign officials ineligible for entry into the country offers one means by which democracies should seek to deter such interference.[19] Democracies should ensure that individual officials shown to have implemented or been responsible for coercive acts over exercises of civil liberties abroad are disqualified from entering or investing within their borders. Against the backdrop of rising US–China tensions, which is likely to impact PRC officials' access to the US, the potential deterrent effect of such measures if introduced in other liberal democracies has increased. The specific intent behind such policies should be clearly communicated to the government in questions through diplomatic channels. Prior to this, governments should issue formal diplomatic protests against any such coercion against lawful political activities. In turn, establishing a national rights monitor accessible to diverse communities would increase the information and evidence base for such measures.

Establish a National Rights Monitor

Governments should establish public-facing rights protection offices to handle cases of foreign interference against civil rights and provide support for members of the community affected. Dirk van der Kley of think tank China Matters has proposed a 'Foreign Interference Commissioner' to be established within the Australian Human Rights Commission.[20] This proposal would similarly help to counter the relative neglect of civil liberties aspects of counter-interference strategy in Australia. For members of diaspora communities experiencing extra-territorial harassment, the new entity could also provide:

- Advice for mitigating or countering coercion or harassment.
- Explanation of relevant laws or sanctioning processes (see above) and the kinds of evidence that might be required to apply them.
- Strategies for helping at-risk family members living abroad.
- Advice on navigating bureaucratic processes, such as law enforcement or immigration.

Such an entity would probably be best situated within human rights commissions or multicultural affairs departments – though this would not preclude referrals to security agencies where appropriate. A national rights monitor would help to control the risk of interference with political freedoms by enabling those concerned to insulate themselves from the source of threat.

---

[19] Author interview with scholar and activist, Princeton, April 2018; author interview with activist, Washington, DC, June 2018.
[20] Van Der Kley, 'What Should Australia Do About … The Influence of United Front Work?'; Pearson, 'Australia's Government Must Guard Against Foreign Interference, But Not by Curbing Our Rights'.

Fund Independent Chinese-Language Media

To substitute the supply of politically sanitised information, liberal-democratic governments must ensure there is funding for independent Chinese-language journalism commensurate with the size and linguistic features of their diaspora populations. This could be delivered by introducing or expanding the Chinese-language services of existing local media, funding initiatives catering to local diaspora communities. In seeking to offset the current pro-PRC skew in diaspora media platforms, governments should be careful to support independent platforms rather than the already well-funded Falun Gong media. Such efforts should also be treated as investments in domestic civil society, rather than foreign policy initiatives, as was the case in the short-lived 'Decode China' project initiated by the US State Department in 2020.[21] Amidst intensifying US–China geopolitical tensions, initiatives to improve Chinese-language information for diaspora communities will need to be critical, impartial and oriented towards local concerns.

Censorship Disclosure Requirements

There is no obvious way to eliminate the risk of media organisations' content being censored when delivered over PRC-based platforms, notably WeChat and TikTok, since the hosting company may have obligations to comply with censorship directives. However, media regulations or guidelines could help to mitigate the impact on news consumers' access to reliable political information. Local news services using foreign platforms could be required to inform their audiences when there has been foreign censorship, and maintain a publicly accessible depository of such content. This would serve to uphold principles of transparency, and potentially put increased attention on the issues that have been omitted from the censored information.

Clear Legal Definitions of State-Led Political Action

Distinguishing different modes of mobilisation is essential for liberal democracies to control the twin risks to civil liberties from suppressive state-led actions and overreaching policy responses.[22] Demonstrations

---

[21] John Power, 'Decode China: US Pulls Plug on Chinese-Language News Site for Australia Without Explanation', *South China Morning Post*, 7 August 2020.

[22] Prominent commentators have called for specific measures against CCP supporters for pro-PRC advocacy. Clive Hamilton, for example, proposes to deny Australian residency to 'any Chinese student who engages in political agitation on behalf of Beijing', with no suggestion that this should apply to any other student group. See Hamilton, *Silent Invasion*, p. 229. Australia's most listened-to radio

that do not interfere with others' rights to political expression are normal exercises of core democratic rights. Where they are carried out with material support or direction of a foreign government, it is appropriate that the organisers publicly register and declare this.[23] Provided the registration process is not onerous, this is a reasonable condition for accepting the advantages of state sponsorship or organisational support. Such a requirement would also help avoid unfair assumptions that pro-PRC actions are covertly state-directed or otherwise illegitimate.

Suppressive counter-protests, by contrast, impinge on the rights of others to political expression. Particular problems include various new technologically enabled methods where intimidation and suppression can happen, such as obtrusive filming and online harassment, as well as the fact that in protest situations sheer numbers can potentially intimidate and interfere with other people's exercise of civil rights. Local security and police should be trained in the management of such situations with explicit regard to the goal of ensuring each side can exercise their rights to political expression and assembly. Violent conduct should be subject to normal law enforcement procedures, and serious criminal penalties should apply for acts of suppressive interference conducted on behalf of a foreign government.[24]

---

host Alan Jones has called for the summary deportation of Chinese students who dare to challenge their Australian lecturers: 'Chinese students are bullying their Australian lecturers at our universities. Cancel their visas and send them all back to China today'. See Fish, 'Hostile Rhetoric Toward Chinese International Students'.

[23] Australia's FITS Law requires registration for political communication 'on behalf of foreign principals on 'a decision of any kind in relation to any matter, including administrative, legislative and policy matters … whether or not the decision is a formal decision'. This could potentially apply to the expression of any kind of support for – or against – any foreign cause about which the Australian government could conceivably adopt a policy. See FITS Law 12(1), 12(2), 12(4). 'Communications activity' is defined as the 'communicat[ion] or distribut[ion of] information or material to the public or a section of the public', including verbally. See FITS Law 13(1) and 13(2). The December 2017 Explanatory Memorandum that accompanied the law's first draft contained an offhand suggestion that a political protest aimed on behalf of a foreign principal might be intended to be registrable where organised by 'a group of persons [who] formed an association' (para. 73).

[24] Under Australia's EFI Law, the current maximum penalty for interference with 'Australian political right or duty' on behalf of a 'foreign principal' is a 20-year jail term. Absent the involvement of a 'foreign principal', the law still prohibits 'violence', 'intimidation' or 'threats' that interfere with the exercise of 'an Australian democratic or political right or duty', with a penalty of up to three years' jail. See EFI Law, 92.2(1) and 83.4(1). As no foreign state involvement is necessary, this could put more commonly accepted forms of suppressive activism, for example, student groups attempting to disrupt Nazi speakers on university campuses, on the wrong side of the law. However, the new law has

Affirm Political Participation of Chinese Communities

To control the risk of overheated public policy debates exacerbating low rates of political participation among Chinese diaspora communities, politicians and officials must strongly affirm the rights of people of all backgrounds to participate in public life. Australia's secretary of the Department of Foreign Affairs and Trade, Frances Adamson, in comments directed at Chinese international students in October 2017, expressed some important nuances: 'No doubt there will be times when you encounter things which to you are unusual, unsettling, or perhaps seem plain wrong … So when you do, let me encourage you not to silently withdraw, or blindly condemn, but to respectfully engage'.[25]

Other leaders and officials should similarly affirm the rights of all residents of liberal democracies to participate in public affairs, in the process taking the opportunity to increase their engagement with Chinese diaspora communities. Doing so not only stands to strengthen government–community relations that enhance social cohesion and bring associated benefits to national security. It would also reduce the need for candidates from the Chinese diaspora community to rely on support from PRC state-aligned community organisations.

Promote Precise Language in Public Discourse

Preventing the fanning of racism and hostility towards PRC migrants and students, and ethnic Chinese and Asian diaspora communities more broadly, requires political leaders, pundits and media organisations to substitute imprecise terms for accurate and measured language. 'Chinese' should not be used interchangeably with 'PRC' or 'CCP'; 'influence' should refer to actual effects; 'operations' should refer to organised, coordinated actions, not individual or spontaneous ones; 'agents' should refer to people acting with another entity's material support or direction; and 'infiltration' or 'covert' should not be used to describe activities, including those of United Front-affiliated organisations and individuals, that are in fact conducted in public.

Avoid Invoking Racism as a Deflection

While affirming diaspora communities' participation in public life and rejecting racial prejudice, it is important that politicians engage and explain substantive issues regarding the PRC political activities. There

---

not yet been tested in court, leaving the exact meaning of terms such as 'intimidation' and 'Australian democratic or political right or duty' unclear.

[25] Frances Adamson, speech at the Confucius Institute Annual Lecture: Australia and China in the 21st Century, University of Adelaide, 7 October 2017.

have been numerous media storms over politicians' affiliations with United Front-aligned community groups. However, despite this, politicians have rarely taken the opportunity to explain the nature of such groups and their role in local community politics, choosing instead to deflect criticism by reference to sensational media coverage. This tactic leaves both legitimate questions and problematic public discourse unaddressed. In 2019, Australian Prime Minister Scott Morrison repeatedly responded to questions over government MP Gladys Liu's affiliations with pro-PRC groups by accusing critics of racism. As Osmond Chiu has noted, this made it difficult 'to highlight the actual racist undertones of some comments about Liu'.[26] The absence of straightforward explanations from Morrison, Liu and other politicians at the centre of media storms over associations with United Front-affiliated groups has, in turn, fed alarmist narratives of infiltration of the political system.

Academic Freedom

Upholding academic freedom in the context of a more powerful and assertive Beijing requires offsetting educational institutions' financial vulnerabilities to the PRC market. The key sources of leverage against such vulnerabilities are information and coordination. Information measures offset risks through the transmission of information to particular groups. Examples include: bolstering China literacy among key personnel; annual public reporting on challenges to academic freedom; establishing clear prohibitions on infringements against academic freedom of students and staff, such as punitive disclosures and suppressive counter-protest; and transparency in contractual arrangements establishing educational partnerships. Coordination measures reduce financial dependence by enabling institutions to find 'safety in numbers', or by outsourcing responsibility to government regulation. Given the imperative of institutional autonomy from government, the first type of coordination measure is generally preferable from the point of view of academic freedom. Examples of coordination measures could include: agreements on standardised annual public reporting practices on free-speech challenges; simultaneous reviews of codes of conduct and associated information-sharing; collective insistence on the above-mentioned transparent contractual arrangements for educational partnership; and cross-institutional solidarity for China researchers.

---

[26] Osmond Chiu, 'Left Out? On Why the Australian Left Struggles When it Comes to China', *The Tocsin* (No. 8, 2019), pp. 25–27, <twitter.com/redrabbleroz/status/1184619753907769344/>, accessed 2 April 2021.

Enhance Management China Literacy

Offsetting the risks of institutional exposure to PRC education markets will require strong China literacy among key personnel. All China-engaged university managers need to bring a critical understanding of the politics of education in the PRC and more broadly in Greater China. This should specifically include the opportunities and constraints that face PRC research institutions, academics and international students, in order to effectively negotiate the increasingly complex environment of international education. Such programmes should draw together: institutions' existing China expertise; external expert briefings, including advice from government; direct engagement and consultation with Chinese researchers and students; and institutional information-sharing mechanisms such as cross-departmental China strategy groups. Governments should also help academic institutions systematically assess their vulnerability to the PRC market.

Annual Reporting on Academic Freedom Challenges

Institutions should report annually on challenges to academic freedom they encounter from all sources, including home governments, foreign states, domestic donors, local and overseas students, and transnational business. Doing so will boost awareness of academic freedom issues by making institutions publicly accountable for appropriately upholding academic freedom, without exposing any one institution to the risk of PRC financial punishment that would place them at a disadvantage to their market competitors. This measure would also facilitate the sharing of experiences and practices across institutions. Eventually, it could pave the way for the development of more or less standard procedures, for example, on how institutions handle demands for curbs on free speech on campus, of which the PRC is by no means the only source.[27]

Review and Summarise Institutional Codes

Codified protections for academic freedom are often dispersed across various policies, rules, codes, charters and other documents, meaning each university's framework is unique and difficult to discern precisely.[28] An independent review of freedom of expression in Australian

---

[27] The suggestion of a standard procedure appears in Lloyd-Damnjanovic, 'A Preliminary Study of PRC Political Influence and Interference Activities in American Higher Education', p. 120.

[28] A non-exhaustive list of relevant documents in Australian universities runs to 33 pages. French, 'Report of the Independent Review of Freedom of Speech in Australian Higher Education Providers', Appendices 4–6.

universities has recommended the adoption of a voluntary 'model code', establishing freedom of speech and academic freedom as 'paramount' and 'defining' values respectively.[29] In the UK, academics have drafted a Model Code of Conduct for the Protection of Academic Freedom and the Academic Community in the Context of the Internationalisation of the UK Higher Education Sector.[30] Regardless of the extent to which they choose to follow such proposals, universities should review their existing policy frameworks to better control risks to academic freedom in light of contemporary political, economic, demographic and technological developments. At a minimum, institutions need to provide accessible summaries of how their various rules relating to academic freedom fit together, and points of contact for members of the university community to seek help on such matters.[31]

At present, few institutions' frameworks appear to address the dynamics of mobilisation and counter-mobilisation that can result in one side's protest being silenced or drowned out.[32] Many also do not explicitly prohibit coercion on the basis of political expression or activity, relying instead on generic policies against intimidation, harassment, bullying, and requirements for conduct to align with concepts of

---

[29] Key proposals include a detailed definition of the meaning of academic freedom; identification of an institutional duty to ensure 'that no member of staff and no student is subject to threatening or intimidating behaviour' due to political expression; legitimate restriction on freedom of speech that would interfere with others' exercise of the same freedom; the need for 'reasonable steps to minimise' any adverse effect of third-party contracts and donations on academic freedom; and the conditionality of academic freedom protections on their not 'fall[ing] below scholarly standards to such an extent as to be detrimental to the university's characters as an institution of higher learning'. See French, 'Report of the Independent Review of Freedom of Speech in Australian Higher Education Providers', pp. 230–36.

[30] Human Rights Consortium, School of Advanced Study, University of London, 'Model Code of Conduct', 2019, <https://hrc.sas.ac.uk/networks/academic-freedom-and-internationalisation-working-group/model-code-conduct>, accessed 22 March 2021.

[31] Human Rights Watch, 'Resisting Chinese Government Efforts to Undermine Academic Freedom Abroad: A Code of Conduct for Colleges, Universities, and Academic Institutions Worldwide', 21 March 2019, <https://www.hrw.org/sites/default/files/supporting_resources/190321_china_academic_freedom_coc_0.pdf>, accessed 7 June 2021.

[32] Counter-protests have been addressed in some UK university policies, such as Lancaster University's 'Code of Conduct on Protests', which stipulates that in the event of competing demonstrations, 'the ability of all sides to safely and effectively express their views will be a primary consideration' (section 16). See <https://www.lancaster.ac.uk/media/lancaster-university/content-assets/documents/strategic-planning–governance/publication-scheme/5-our-policies-and-procedures/Code-of-conduct-protests.pdf>, accessed 22 March 2021.

academic or intellectual freedom.[33] Higher education institutions' codes and frameworks – or their summaries – should clearly prohibit suppressive mobilisation, as well as any threats or intimidation on the basis of political views. Institutions should also consider prohibitions on the use of cameras or other technologies in obtrusive or intimidatory ways, particularly during public speech events.

'Chatham House Light' Rule on Campus

Punitive and coercive disclosures – the reporting of lawful comments or activities that would place any person at risk of coercion or punishment – must be clearly prohibited within university settings. The 'Chatham House Rule' of non-attribution of remarks made in specified settings offers one possible model. Universities and academics should introduce standard language into codes of conduct and course outlines – as is commonly done for plagiarism and cheating – establishing that punitive disclosure of a person's statements or actions in a university constitutes misconduct. For example, this could read:

> Disclosure of classroom speech: UK law and international conventions require universities to maintain an environment of academic freedom for all members of the university community. Accordingly, disclosure of another person's lawful speech or activity that would place any other person at risk of harm will be treated as misconduct, for which penalties ranging up to expulsion may apply. Any person with concerns over potential harmful disclosures should consult the course convenor [and other relevant institutional contacts].

This is a control measure designed to place distance between sources and the subject of the risk; it will not guarantee that such disclosures never occur, but an express prohibition would be likely to reduce their incidence.[34] The most important function of such standard language, however, would be to reassure all students and staff of their right to an academic environment

---

[33] For example, University of Melbourne, 'Student Conduct Policy', <policy.unimelb.edu.au/MPF1324>, accessed 2 April 2021; University of Western Australia, 'Code of Conduct', <www.hr.uwa.edu.au/policies/policies/conduct/code/conduct>, accessed 12 July 2021; University of Western Australia, 'University Charter of Student Rights and Responsibilities', <https://www.uwa.edu.au/policy/home>, accessed 22 March 2021; University of Sydney, 'Student Charter 2020', <sydney.edu.au/policies/showdoc.aspx?recnum=PDOC2011/215&RendNum=0>, accessed 22 March 2021.

[34] On the supply side, overseas students who maintain contact with foreign state authorities may be less inclined to make such disclosures if they are explicitly forbidden. On the demand side, organisationally risk-averse CCP officials may be less inclined to an activity that is expressly prohibited.

free from the threat of harmful disclosure, and the availability of assistance for those experiencing concerns of political interference.

Enhance Support Services for International Students

Many higher-education providers generate significant income from international students, but unsatisfactory experiences are common, particularly among those from the PRC.[35] Institutions should be required to set aside a proportion of international revenue streams to support services to ensure the welfare of all international students. These should account for the particular challenges they may face in areas such as cultural differences, language abilities and mental health, as well as political issues. Ideally, universities would agree among themselves regarding the appropriate proportion of this lucrative income stream to be set aside for specialised international student welfare, but if self-regulation fails, governments could use regulatory frameworks to mandate it in order to place their higher-education export industries on a sustainable footing and protect their country's reputation as a destination for study.

Specific initiatives for enhancing support services for international students should be identified through an evidence-based process, starting with student feedback surveys and/or focus groups, expert advice and consultation with alumni networks, but might include:

- Increasing numbers of language-capable staff and guidance for accessing student welfare and academic support services.
- Designated, easily accessible points of contact in key offices such as student unions and faculty support offices.
- New programmes facilitating greater interaction between international and local students.
- Training of staff in how to run cross-cultural discussions.[36]
- Making key orientation content available in overseas students' first language, particularly subjects such as academic culture, campus politics, local laws and key university policies, including those regarding free speech and academic freedom.
- Increased campus security where necessary to ensure free speech for all sides when contending political mobilisations occur.

---

[35] Jakobson and Gill, 'Is There A Problem with Chinese International Students?', pp. 2–3.
[36] Fran Martin, 'Why Universities Should Invest More to Support Chinese Students', in Philipp Ivanov (ed.), *Disruptive Asia 2019: China Special Edition* (Sydney: Asia Society, 2019).

Enhanced specialist support services would elevate the quality of the university experience for international students and students in general. For PRC students, such measures would reduce dependence on services provided by Beijing, and potentially dampen the appeal of nationalist activism which can be driven by a sense of isolation and marginalisation from local society.[37]

Transparency of Contracts and Arrangements

CIs can bring significant benefits to communities by providing opportunities for Chinese language learning. However, as discussed in Chapter II, opaque contractual arrangements between universities and CIs challenge academic freedom, while also precluding assessment of the nature and severity of any threats and inviting speculation as to their possible content. CI contractual arrangements should be made public and their activities should be subject to normal faculty oversight.[38] The prospect of CIs teaching for-credit university courses, especially courses on contemporary China, presents particular risks to academic freedom as well as educational standards, and should be avoided and, where already in place, phased out.[39] Language learning, by contrast, does not depend on politically balanced teaching materials to provide net benefits.

Institutional Support for China Researchers

Surveys have found a significant minority of China researchers face risks of repression in the conduct of their study, and many do not feel they can obtain support from their institutions in dealing with the PRC government.[40] Universities should develop cross-institutional agreements facilitating collective representations on behalf of their academics to the PRC government. More broadly, research institutions, including think tanks, should seek to develop a consensus-based code of conduct, focused on voluntary standards of transparency, for researchers in their

---

[37] See Helen Gao, 'Chinese, Studying in America, and Struggling', *New York Times*, 12 December 2017.

[38] Kwok, 'Is There A Problem With … Confucius Institutes?'.

[39] As Perry Link points out: 'If we rule out not just June Fourth but all the other "sensitive" issues – Xinjiang, Tibet, Taiwan, Falun Gong, Occupy Central, the Nobel Peace Prize, the spectacular private wealth of leaders' families, the cynical arrests of rights advocates and sometimes their deaths in prisons, and more – we are left with a picture of China that is not only smaller than the whole but crucially different in nature'. See Robert Kapp et al., 'The Debate Over Confucius Institutes', ChinaFile, 23 July 2014, <https://www.chinafile.com/conversation/debate-over-confucius-institutes>, accessed 2 April 2021.

[40] Greitens and Truex, 'Repressive Experiences Among China Scholars', p. 20.

Figure 6: Disaggregated Issues and Policy Suggestions

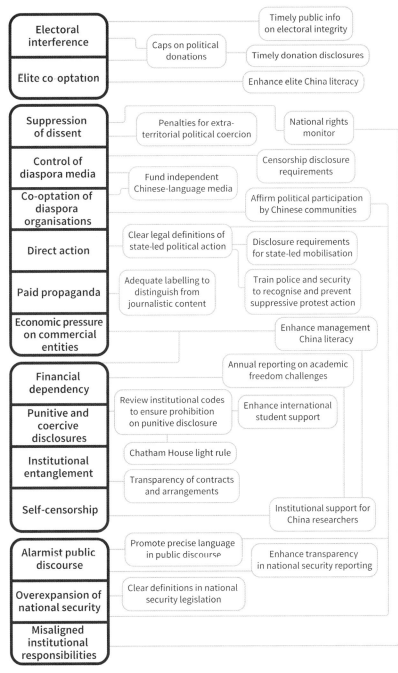

Source: Author generated.

dealings with politically sensitive matters overseas, again leveraging 'safety in numbers'.[41]

Conclusion

As the various interlocking policy measures suggested in this chapter demonstrate, disaggregating and managing the distinct risks that PRC overseas political activities present does not mean approaching the issues in isolation from one another. It clearly also does not imply adopting a permissive stance towards PRC interference that threatens the security of the political system, the civil rights of individuals and at-risk groups, or the principles of academic freedom that are supposed to underpin liberal universities. Nor does it mean divorcing the issues from the larger context of the PRC's increasing authoritarianism or the emerging political systems competition. The strength of liberal democracy in a protracted contest of ideas will depend on addressing these challenges in a methodical manner consistent with those ideals. Still less does disaggregation and risk management require blindness to the PRC's own political strategies and their political-philosophical premises. But while studying and taking account of the CCP's strategies and ideas is crucial to the development of policy responses – especially in executive education – it is equally important to avoid internalising Beijing's view of politics in the process, as the Conclusion argues.

---

[41] See Benner et al., 'Authoritarian Advance', p. 42; Geremie Barmé et al., 'Resistance and the Ethical China Watcher', *China Heritage*, 22 June 2018.

CONCLUSION: TWO 'WORLD OUTLOOKS'

In his 1937 essay, 'On Contradiction', Mao Zedong wrote of two opposing 'world outlooks'.[1] One was the correct 'materialist dialectical' view that takes all phenomena in the natural and social worlds to be the outcome of contradictions. The other was the incorrect 'metaphysical' view affirming the existence of transcendent properties such as truth and natural rights. Developed by CCP ideologists over subsequent decades, the idea that all political developments result from clashes between two opposing forces continues to suffuse CCP theory and policy.[2] It is a view of politics that leaves no room for individual human agency, principled middle ground or actions taken in good faith. It renders human intentions irrelevant in the understanding of political actions, whose character is instead defined by which 'force' they form part of – that is, which side of the 'contradiction' they are on – at the particular time they occur.[3]

A 2013 film produced by a PLA propaganda unit and leaked online reminded observers of the ongoing dominance of the materialist-dialectical world outlook in Beijing in Xi's 'New Era'. Titled *Silent Contest* (较量无声), the film depicted a vast conspiracy among Western governments, civil society and citizens coordinating consciously or

---

[1] Mao Zedong, 'On Contradiction', in *Selected Works of Mao Tse-tung, Volume I* (Beijing: Foreign Languages Press, 1937/1965), pp. 311–47; see also Mao Zedong, 'On the Correct Handling of Contradictions Among the People', in *Selected Works of Mao Tse-tung, Volume V* (Beijing: Foreign Languages Press, 1957/1977), pp. 384–422.

[2] See Heath, *China's New Governing Party Paradigm*.

[3] As the Sinologist Pierre Ryckmans (whose pen-name was Simon Leys) once noted: 'Dialectics is the jolly art that enables the Supreme Leader never to make mistakes – for even if he did the wrong thing, he did it at the right time, which makes it right for him to have been wrong, whereas the Enemy, even if he did the right thing, did it at the wrong time, which makes it wrong for him to have been right'. See Simon Leys, 'The Art of Reading Nonexistent Inscriptions Written in Invisible Ink on a Blank Page', in *The Hall of Uselessness: Collected Essays* (New York, NY: NYRB, 2013), eBook version, pp. 844–45.

unconsciously (the distinction was irrelevant) to infiltrate and subvert China's rise under the CCP.[4] A similar mode of thinking has, ironically, also gained ground within policy discussions on the PRC's overseas political activities in liberal democracies. The parallels between *Silent Contest* and the influential Australian polemic *Silent Invasion* run deep, and are far from a lone example.[5] As the US–China geostrategic rivalry intensifies, for many politicians and commentators, words and actions perceived to suit Beijing's purposes are increasingly conflated with the work of the party-state itself.[6]

The PRC under Xi has – so far – proved to be a repressive and increasingly authoritarian Leninist party-state with an expanding set of interests overseas, and a growing array of capabilities to advance them. But in studying and taking account of the CCP's political strategies, liberal democracies must be careful to avoid accepting the party's orthodox view of the world. Aggregating the array of risks presented by the PRC's overseas political activities into a CCP-orchestrated campaign of subversion not only aligns with the 'materialist-dialectical' view of politics, it also plays into the CCP's hands politically. It inflates the CCP's ability to control the domestic politics of liberal democracies, sharpening internal divisions and obscuring opportunities to address institutional shortcomings. It propounds a divisive vision of a world of 'hostile foreign forces' and fifth columns, and takes far too seriously Beijing's claims on the loyalty of ethnic Chinese worldwide. Politicians and commentators aiming to defend liberal democracy should be clear about which of the two 'world outlooks' they are adopting as they grapple with these complex challenges.

---

[4] *Silent Contest* (Part One), <www.youtube.com/watch?v=rskYCubTSvE>; *Silent Contest* (Part Two), <www.youtube.com/watch?v=czI9GKiTKZg>. For an English-language transcript, see <chinascope.org/archives/6447/92> (Part One) and <chinascope.org/main/content/view/6168/92> (Part Two), accessed 22 March 2021.

[5] Others include Rob Spalding, *Stealth War: How China Took Over While America's Elite Slept* (New York, NY: Portfolio, 2019); Clive Hamilton and Mareike Ohlberg, *Hidden Hand: Exposing How the Chinese Communist Party is Reshaping the World* (London: Oneworld, 2020).

[6] For example, the foreign editor of a major Australian daily suggested academics who criticised draft national security laws and alarmism were wittingly or unwittingly taking part in a 'weaponised narrative' attack designed 'to muddy the discussion in Australia and undercut Australia's ability to defend its sovereignty'. See Chris Zappone, 'Is Talk of Australia's "Anti-China" Bias a Weaponised Narrative?', *The Age*, 19 May 2018; Chris Uhlmann, one of Australia's best-known journalists, interpreted it as a sign that 'our academic class have been recruited by money to parrot the lines of Beijing'. See Louisa Lim, 'Stranger than Spy Fiction', Los Angeles Review of Books China Channel, 27 September 2018, <https://chinachannel.org/2018/09/27/hanopticon>, accessed 22 March 2021.

There are numerous ways liberal democracies can, and should, address the issues covered in this paper without necessarily resorting to the pursuit of security at the expense of liberty. Options for addressing the issues raised by PRC overseas political activities are at least as many as the issues themselves. A prerequisite for generating maximally effective policy measures is the careful disaggregation of this diverse array of problems.